500

tapas

500

tapas

the only tapas compendium you'll ever need

María Segura

SELLERS
PUBLISHING

A Quintet Book

Published by Sellers Publishing, Inc.
161 John Roberts Road, South Portland, Maine 04106
Visit our Web site: www.sellerspublishing.com
E-mail: rsp@rsvp.com

ISBN: 978-1-4162-0653-8
Library of Congress Control Number: 2011935635
QTT.FTAP

This book was conceived, designed, and produced by
Quintet Publishing Limited
6 Blundell Street
London N7 9BH
United Kingdom

Food Stylist: Georgie Besterman
Photographer: Ian Garlick
Art Director: Michael Charles
Editorial Assistant: Holly Willsher
Managing Editor: Donna Gregory
Publisher: Mark Searle

10 9 8 7 6 5 4 3 2 1

Printed in China by 1010 Printing International Ltd.

contents

introduction 6

para picar (light tapas) 16

tapas variadas (mixed tapas) 40

pescado y mariscos (seafood tapas) 70

pollo y pato (poultry tapas) 100

tapas de puerco (pork tapas) 126

tapas de cordero (lamb tapas) 150

tapas de carne (beef tapas) 176

tapas exóticas (game tapas) 202

tapas de vegetales (vegetable tapas) 228

tapas dulces (dessert tapas) 256

index 282

introduction

What could be more evocatively Spanish than to take refuge from the sun with a fortifying drink and to nibble at some fresh, tastebud-tingling, perfect tapas? Tradition holds that tapas was originally a slice of bread or ham used as a lid to keep insects out of drinks, hence the speculation that "tapas" is derived from the verb *tapar*, "to cover."

However it started, tapas is now a staple of the Spanish bar experience, where mouthfuls of delicious treats, mostly on toasts or carvings of bread, are served with traditional toppings like morcilla and piquillo peppers or pâtés and cured meats with capers.

Yet this is by no means where tapas ends. The notion of perfect and delicious little bar snacks has now taken wing from its humble beginnings, developing into a worldwide gastronomic delight perceptively different from the usual restaurant experience. Still essentially Spanish in its compositions of herbs, seasonings, and ingredients, tapas has become more luxurious and decadent while still maintaining the feel of convivial food.

Now that the popularity of tapas has become a worldwide trend, it is possible to observe an evolution in its styles. It has become feasible to take almost any popular meal, minimize it down to a single tasting-sized portion, and presto, a new tapas has sprung from the void. In this book you will find examples of this, such as a ballotine of rabbit on white beans, and lightly spiced quail pieces with a pomegranate sauce.

Tapas and the dynamic of sharing food has created an amazing assortment of large, one-pot dishes, specially styled as a focal point, around which a group can sit and chat, scooping off mouthful-sized portions as the mood takes them. Such examples of this are slow-roasted

marinated lamb kebabs with zesty fava beans, page 164

lamb shoulder with pomegranate salad, and crisped pork belly with slow-cooked beans. Can you imagine a more enticing shared delight than a party pulling apart these aromatic and tender meats in good company with excellent wine?

The other style to emerge in tapas is what to all intents and purposes appears to be a large plated serving of food — a meal for one. On further inspection, these dishes are always cunningly created to be shared — such as a rare ribeye steak served with polenta fries and piquillo peppers, or a beautifully pan-fried piece of chicken in a nest of truffled gnocchi. Certainly it's more fun to have lots of plates on the table and sample a little from each than to have just one large meal to oneself.

Tapas is all about sharing in so many ways. It is not just a food genre, it is a means for gathering and convening, of drinking wine, talking, and indulging together on something that is just a little bit special. I hope you have a wonderful time exploring the world of tapas with *500 Tapas*.

ingredients

olive oil
Spanish olive oils are unique. They have a deepness and richness unlike many others and are such an important part in Spanish cooking. I would find a good light one for simple frying and cooking, and a really good extra-virgin olive oil for dipping, making dressings, emulsions, and richer sauces.

smoked paprika
Smoked paprika is one of the most Spanish of all the spices. Its bright red color just screams Spain! Spanish paprika (*pimentón*) is available in three versions — mild (pimentón dulce), moderately spicy (*pimentón agridulce*), and very spicy (pimentón picante).

saffron
Saffron is a spice that is simply the stamen of the saffron crocus. It is the most expensive spice in the world. It has a soapy bitter taste when used in abundance and dyes the food bright yellow, but used sparingly it adds a warmth and aroma to a dish.

piquillo peppers
The piquillo pepper is a variety of chile traditionally grown in northern Spain. Its name is derived from the Spanish for "little beak." These peppers are roasted over embers, which gives them a distinct sweet, spicy flavor, more similar to bell peppers than chile peppers, despite their small size. They are then peeled and seeded by hand, before being packed into jars.

pimientos de padrón
Pimientos de Padrón are small green peppers roughly the size of your thumb. They're fried in olive oil, salted, and served at many tapas bars in Spain. Besides being salty and sweet, most

puree de habas, page 41

people eat pimientos de Padrón for the fun of it. Eating them is considered a form of culinary Russian roulette. Some are sweet. Others are hot enough to blow your mind!

membrillo

This quince jelly is wonderful with cheeses, game, or pâté, and it also works well spread with roasted meats and whipped up into aïoli.

chorizo

Chorizo is a sausage that comes either fresh or semidry, in which case it must be cooked before eating, or as a sausage that has been cured and hung. Spanish chorizo gets its distinctive smokiness and deep red color from paprika. It is the heart of many Spanish dishes.

charcuterie with pickled garlic & caper berries, page 20

morcilla

Morcilla is a Spanish black pudding or blood sausage. What makes it different from other blood sausages is that it has more texture from its rice filling and is a little spicier. For those who aren't sure about eating blood pudding, try morcilla. It's one of the best in the world.

anchovies

Salted or vinegared anchovies are a staple of the Spanish diet. If using the salted variety, they can be added to dishes to add seasoning. If you don't think you're a fan, still give them a try. They can be the backbone to the most authentic Spanish flavor.

capers & caperberries

Capers are the unripened flower buds of *Capparis spinosa*. After the buds are harvested, they are dried in the sun, then pickled in vinegar, brine, or salt. The curing brings out their tangy lemony flavor, much the same as green olives. You find them in various sizes from tiny balls, which add punch, to the more grown-up caper berries that are not quite as interesting but add drama to your dish.

sherry (fino)

Sherry is as big in Spain as wine. In Spanish cooking you would be as likely to find a good sherry in your food as you would wine. A good dry fino would be the store cupboard essential I would recommend, but there are some recipes that call for the super thick and sweet Pedro Ximénez and also a richer amontillado.

sherry vinegar

With sherry's popularity in Spain, it is the vinegar of choice too. In the same way the Italians credit their balsamic, the Spanish take great pride in their sherry vinegars. You will find them in many different qualities. As with oils, get the best you can afford.

equipment

One of the many joys of tapas is that very little specialty equipment is essential. There are just a very few pieces that will make your homemade tapas experience a little more authentic, but to start with, you can certainly make do with whatever is already in your kitchen. Should you wish to invest, here are a selection of dishes and pans that will be wonderful additions to your kitchen.

paella pan
Spanish food wouldn't be Spanish food without a good paella pan. These pans are classically made from polished steel, but now you can find a wide variety in all sorts of shapes and sizes from stainless steel to nonstick to cast-iron. Now they are even made for induction cooktops. The paella in this book is to feed four people, so a smaller pan, about 12 inches in diameter, would be ideal.

mini tortilla pan
Small tortilla pans may seem like a luxury, but the small tortilla recipe in this book outweighs larger tortillas for flavor and freshness, and you can undercook them a little easier, giving that luscious gooey middle.

earthenware tapas dishes
Earthenware is what you would classically find tapas in. It is the perfect material. You can bake with it, and it keeps your food hot and in individual portions. I would get a selection of sizes, as you can use smaller ones for olives and nuts and larger ones for the more substantial dishes. The classic size is around 4 1/2 to 6 inches.

paella with seafood & chicken, page 86

chicken with potatoes, olives & sherry, page 111

ovenproof ceramic dishes
As an alternative to earthenware, you can have a selection of dishes made from glazed ceramic — anything from the size and depth of a ramekin to a shorter wider variety.

wooden boards
As charcuterie is such a major part of the tapas culture, having a beautiful wooden board for serving cold meats on is a must for tapas.

wooden kebab skewers
The idea of tapas is that it's a mouthful of food, and what easier way of making tasty mouthfuls than serving dishes as kebabs. I would suggest small lengths, maybe long enough to fit two or three pieces of meat, fish, or vegetables.

toothpicks
Go into any tapas bar in Madrid and the bread tapas will be held together with toothpicks. There will be toothpicks to pick up your olives. Toothpicks to skewer things. A box of toothpicks will never go unused when serving your tapas.

mortar & pestle
When dealing with spices and aromatics, having a good sturdy mortar and pestle around to pound flavor into food is essential. I like the gravel-textured ones that are really heavy.

para picar
light tapas

Tiny munchy little nibbles, para picar are light and tempting. The whole idea being that these little treats can be plucked from a dish with the fingers or skewed on a cocktail stick. No cutlery is ever needed.

marinated olives

see variations page 32

This is such an easy way to jazz up olives — the most familiar of tapas nibbles. Once marinated, the aromatic spices and herbs marry perfectly with the firm salty olives, creating an elegant little dish that will have you reaching for more.

1/2 tsp. cumin seeds
1/2 tsp. fennel seeds
5 dried chiles (pequín variety, if possible)
3 cloves garlic, peeled and left whole
1 lemon, sliced

1 large sprig fresh rosemary
1 (12-oz.) jar Spanish unstuffed green, black,
    or mixed olives in brine or olive oil, drained
1/3 cup really good Spanish extra-virgin
    olive oil

Place the cumin and fennel seeds and chiles in a small skillet and toast over low heat for 1 minute or until they start to become aromatic. Put them into a mixing bowl along with all the other ingredients. Mix well, then transfer into a large lidded jar and let marinate in the refrigerator for 1–2 days before serving. These must be eaten within 2 weeks.

Serves 4

roasted almonds & seeds

see variations page 33

This is a delightful crunchy concoction of nuts and seeds to graze on alongside a glass of wine. If you have concerns about nut allergies, replace the almonds with extra pumpkin and sunflower seeds.

2 cups whole almonds, with skin
1/3 cup pumpkin seeds
1/3 cup sunflower seeds
4 tbsp. olive oil

1 tsp. dried chile pepper flakes
1/2 tsp. cumin seeds
1 tbsp. sea salt
1 tsp. freshly ground black pepper

Preheat the oven to 350°F. Mix all the ingredients together in a bowl. Transfer to a large roasting pan. Cook for 20–25 minutes, turning at regular intervals until the almonds are deep gold. Drain on paper towels and add a little more salt if desired. Serve warm.

Makes 2 2/3 cups

charcuterie with pickled garlic & caper berries

see variations page 34

This is the absolute cornerstone of tapas, a simple but vital centerpiece. It can be easily presented on a wooden board (olive wood is wonderful) at the center of the table and you'll be fighting everyone off to get to it.

8 slices dried chorizo
8 slices Serrano ham
8 slices Spanish ham
8 slices Spanish air-dried sausage

1/2 cup pickled garlic
1/2 cup pickled caper berries
drizzle of really good-quality Spanish
    extra-virgin olive oil

Lay your different charcuterie meats elegantly on a board. Scatter with the pickled garlic and caper berries. Drizzle with olive oil and serve with warm crusty bread.

Serves 4

marinated manchego with peppers & cumin

see variations page 35

Marinating cheese might seem odd, but smooth manchego is complemented deliciously by the piquant cumin and peppers.

1 tsp. cumin seeds
1/2 cup extra-virgin olive oil
sea salt and freshly ground black pepper

12 slices Spanish manchego cheese
1 cup roasted red peppers (jarred, if desired),
    cut into strips

Heat a small dry skillet and toast the cumin seeds for 30 seconds or until they become aromatic. Whisk the seeds into the olive oil with some salt and pepper.

Arrange the cheese slices in an airtight storage container. Pour in the cumin dressing and sprinkle with the pepper strips. Toss to mingle all the ingredients, then refrigerate overnight. Let stand at room temperature for 1 hour before serving in a deep bowl with all the marinade.

Serves 4

boquerones

see variations page 36

Boquerones are tiny butterflied anchovies, in a very acidic marinade that serves to cure the fish as well as add flavor. This recipe can only be done with fresh fish, so the smallest sardines will do if anchovies are not available.

1 1/3 cups fresh anchovies or small sardines,
   4–5 inches long, preferably from Spain
1 tsp. sea salt
3/4 cup white wine vinegar

2 tbsp. fresh lemon juice
3 cloves garlic, crushed
1/2 small bunch fresh parsley, finely chopped

Using your fingers, butterfly the anchovies. Run your finger along the backbone, separating the flesh from the bone as your finger gently slides down to the tail. Then lift out the bones in one piece. Starting with the head, you simply peel the bone away from the flesh — backbone, tail, and all. You are left with a whole, clean, butterflied fillet.

Place the anchovies in an airtight container, skin-side down, and sprinkle them lightly with sea salt. You may need to do this in layers.

Mix the vinegar, lemon juice, garlic, and parsley. Pour the mixture over the fillets. Give the container a shake to cover all the fish with the marinade. Cover the container and refrigerate for 2 days. The fish will marinate and turn white.

Serve piled on a board or plate with a trickle of the marinating liquid.

Serves 4

pan-fried pimientos de padrón

see variations page 37

This is an elementary tapas dish, served with lashings of olive oil and salt in every good tapas bar. To the eye, these small smoky peppers all appear the same, but eating them is a game of gastronomic Russian roulette, as around one in every nine is fiery hot. So dive in with a cool drink in hand in case you happen to pick a feisty one.

1 1/2 cups Spanish green peppers (preferably   2 tbsp. light olive oil
   pimientos de Padrón)   1/2 tsp. sea salt

Wash the peppers thoroughly in cold water and pat dry. Place a large lidded skillet over high heat, add the olive oil, and heat until almost smoking.

Add the peppers, cover, and cook for 4–5 minutes, turning occasionally, until blistered and slightly charred. Drain the peppers on paper towels, sprinkle generously with the sea salt, and serve.

Serves 4

fried chorizo & potatoes

see variations page 38

This crunchy dish is an exciting take on potato chips. Chorizo is an unusual sausage, as it turns deliciously crispy when fried. Just be sure to fry the potatoes first; otherwise, the oils and spices released by the chorizo will stain the potatoes red.

vegetable oil for deep-frying
1 large red-skinned potato, peeled and really
   thinly sliced

2 raw chorizo sausages, sliced thin
1/2 tsp. sea salt

Fill a deep saucepan to half full with vegetable oil and heat to 350°F. In the hot oil, fry the potato slices in batches for 1–2 minutes until golden. Remove with a slotted spoon and drain on paper towels. Repeat with the slices of chorizo, allowing the slices to turn golden and become crisp. Drain on paper towels. Sprinkle the potatoes and the chorizo with salt and serve immediately.

Serves 4

salt cod-stuffed piquillo peppers

see variations page 39

Punchy and piquant, piquillo peppers are a regular feature in Spanish cooking. These scarlet beauties are often found pickled or canned, which makes them a fantastic item to keep in your pantry. When stuffing the peppers, handle them with the utmost care as the skins tear easily, which will ruin their ability to contain the salt cod mixture.

3/4 cup dry salt cod
1 bay leaf
1 potato, a floury variety such as russet, peeled, boiled, and mashed
2 cloves garlic, crushed and finely chopped
zest and juice of 1 lemon

1/2 cup extra-virgin olive oil, plus extra for greasing and drizzling
salt and freshly ground black pepper
4 jarred piquillo peppers (or any other whole red peppers in a jar)

Soak the salt cod in cold water 24 hours in advance, changing the water halfway through.

Preheat oven to 350°F. Place the soaked salt cod in a large pan with cold, fresh water to cover, add the bay leaf, and bring just to the boiling point. Remove pan from heat, set aside, and rest for 5–10 minutes. Remove salt cod from the pan and let cool. When the fish is cool enough to handle, remove any skin or bones and flake the flesh. In a large bowl, mix the fish, potatoes, garlic, and lemon zest and juice together, mashing vigorously with a fork. Add oil bit by bit, slowly beating it into the mixture until absorbed. Season with salt and freshly ground pepper. Fill the peppers with the fish mixture, taking care not to tear the flesh. Place the filled peppers in a lightly oiled baking pan and bake for about 20 minutes, until filling is heated through. Drizzle with olive oil and serve immediately.

Serves 4

marinated olives

see base recipe page 17

marinated olives with thyme & bay leaves
Prepare the basic recipe, replacing the cumin and fennel seeds and dried chiles with 1 teaspoon chopped fresh thyme and 2 bay leaves. Omit the lemon and rosemary.

marinated olives with mint
Prepare the basic recipe, replacing the cumin and fennel seeds, dried chiles, and rosemary with 1 tablespoon chopped fresh mint.

marinated olives with thyme
Prepare the basic recipe, replacing the cumin and fennel seeds and dried chiles with 1 teaspoon chopped fresh thyme.

marinated olives with red peppers & basil
Prepare the basic recipe, replacing the cumin and fennel seeds and rosemary with 1 tablespoon chopped roasted red pepper (from a jar is fine) and 1 tablespoon chopped fresh basil.

variations

roasted almonds & seeds

see base recipe page 19

spicy roasted almonds & seeds
Prepare the basic recipe, replacing the cumin and red pepper flakes with
1/4 teaspoon cayenne pepper and 1/2 teaspoon paprika.

curry-roasted almonds & seeds
Prepare the basic recipe, replacing the cumin and red pepper flakes with
1 teaspoon curry powder.

roasted almonds, seeds & raisins
Prepare the basic recipe, replacing half the seeds with 2 tablespoons golden
raisins.

roasted walnuts, seeds & apricots
Prepare the basic recipe, replacing the almonds with walnut halves, and half
the seeds with 2 tablespoons chopped dried apricots.

charcuterie with pickled garlic & caper berries

see base recipe page 20

charcuterie with red peppers & arugula
Prepare the basic recipe, replacing the garlic and caper berries with
3 thinly sliced roasted red peppers (canned peppers are fine) and decorating
the board with dressed arugula leaves.

salami charcuterie with pickled garlic & caper berries
Prepare the basic recipe, replacing the hams with several varieties of
Italian salami.

pâté charcuterie with pickled garlic & caper berries
Prepare the basic recipe, replacing the hams with several varieties of pâtés.

charcuterie with mortadella, truffle cheese & pistachios
Prepare the basic recipe, replacing the hams with mortadella sausage and
truffle cheese. Omit the garlic and caper berries and serve with peeled
pistachio nuts sprinkled over the sausage.

marinated manchego with peppers & cumin

see base recipe page 23

marinated manchego with caper berries & anchovies
Prepare the basic recipe, replacing the toasted cumin seeds and roasted red peppers with 1 tablespoon caper berries and 4 anchovy fillets.

marinated manchego with basil & tomatoes
Prepare the basic recipe, replacing the toasted cumin seeds and roasted red peppers with 1 tablespoon chopped basil and 1/2 cup chopped cherry tomatoes.

marinated manchego with thyme & garlic
Prepare the basic recipe, replacing the cumin seeds and roasted red peppers with 1 teaspoon chopped fresh thyme and 2 finely sliced garlic cloves.

marinated manchego with wine & tarragon
Prepare the basic recipe, omitting the cumin seeds and roasted red peppers and adding 1 teaspoon chopped fresh tarragon, 1/4 cup white wine, 1 tablespoon white wine vinegar, 1 finely chopped garlic clove, and 1 teaspoon chopped fresh thyme.

variations

boquerones

see base recipe page 24

boquerones with sour cream & dill

Prepare the basic recipe. Before serving, drain the marinated anchovies.
Gently mix in 2 tablespoons sour cream and 1 tablespoon chopped fresh dill.

boquerones with tomatoes & scallions

Prepare the basic recipe, adding 2 finely chopped tomatoes and 2 finely
sliced scallions to the marinade. Mix gently.

boquerones with red pepper

Prepare the basic recipe, adding 1 finely chopped red bell pepper and
1/4 teaspoon cayenne pepper to the marinade.

boquerones with gherkins & capers

Prepare the basic recipe, adding 4 finely chopped small gherkins and
1 tablespoon capers to the marinade.

pan-fried pimientos de padrón

see base recipe page 27

pan-fried garlic pimientos de padrón
Prepare the basic recipe, replacing the sea salt with garlic salt.

pan-fried spicy pimientos de padrón
Prepare the basic recipe, adding 1/2 teaspoon ground cumin to the oil
before cooking.

pan-fried coriander pimientos de padrón
Prepare the basic recipe, adding 1/2 teaspoon ground coriander to the oil
before cooking.

pan-fried pimientos de padrón & fried chorizo
Prepare the basic recipe, adding 1 chopped chorizo sausage to the oil and
frying for 1 minute before adding the peppers.

variations

fried chorizo & potatoes

see base recipe page 28

fried chorizo & parsnips
Prepare the basic recipe, replacing the potato with 2 medium parsnips.

fried chorizo & cumin potatoes
Prepare the basic recipe. Serve with a generous sprinkling of cumin.

fried chorizo & beets
Prepare the basic recipe, replacing the potato with fresh beets. Serve with a
dip of crème fraîche (or soured cream) mixed with 1 tablespoon freshly
chopped chives.

fried chorizo & rosemary potatoes
Prepare the basic recipe, replacing the salt with rosemary salt.

salt cod-stuffed piquillo peppers

see base recipe page 30

piquillo peppers stuffed with shrimp
Prepare the basic recipe, replacing the salt cod with the same amount of
cooked shrimp.

piquillo peppers stuffed with goat cheese
Prepare the basic recipe, omitting the salt cod and garlic. Replace with
a stuffing of the mashed potato combined with 1/2 cup goat cheese,
1/2 teaspoon dried red pepper flakes, 2 finely sliced scallions, and 1 teaspoon
freshly chopped mint.

piquillo peppers stuffed with crabmeat
Prepare the basic recipe, omitting the salt cod. Replace with a stuffing of
the mashed potato combined with 3/4 cup white crabmeat, 1 chopped chile,
1/2 bunch finely chopped fresh cilantro, and the juice of 1 lime.

piquillo peppers stuffed with ham & rice
Prepare the basic recipe, replacing the salt cod and potato stuffing with 1 cup
cooked rice mixed with 1/4 cup chopped ham and 1 teaspoon paprika.

tapas variadas
mixed tapas

Tempting crisp toast or warm fresh bread, served as a platform for smooth tapenades and warm oozy cheese, the combination is irresistible. Breads are also cunningly used to make a crunchy crumb coating around some of these bite-size treats.

puree de habas

see variations page 60

Simply translated, this is a puree of fava beans, but the dish is so much more than that. Imagine sweet, sticky roasted garlic, pureed with fresh rosemary, fava beans, and olive oil, and served hot with crusty bread to spread it on. Simply delicious!

1 whole head garlic
sea salt and freshly ground black pepper
1 1/4 cups olive oil

leaves from 1 sprig fresh rosemary, chopped
1 lb. fresh fava (broad) beans, shelled, and
   boiled under tender

Preheat the oven to 350°F. Cut the top off the garlic, season the exposed cloves with a sprinkle of salt and pepper, place on a baking sheet, drizzle with a little oil, and bake for 25 minutes, until soft to touch.

When cool enough to handle, squeeze the soft center from the garlic and add to a blender along with the rosemary, hot fava beans, salt, and pepper. Blend the ingredients to a fine paste while slowly pouring in the olive oil.

Pour the mixture into a skillet with a splash of water and sauté for 2–3 minutes until heated through and bubbling. Serve in a bowl, drizzled with olive oil, with crusty bread to spread it on.

Serves 4

pan con tomate

see variations page 61

The Italians are renowned for their bruschetta, which is a simple tomato salad on toasted bread that has been rubbed with garlic and olive oil. The Spanish do it differently and, in my opinion, with more flair. The Spanish treat the bread the same, but when it comes to the tomatoes they literally squish really ripe fresh tomatoes into the bread.

4 slices dense rustic bread
2 cloves garlic, halved
2 large, vine-ripened tomatoes, as ripe as
   possible, halved

5 tbsp. really good extra-virgin olive oil
sea salt and freshly ground black pepper

Heat a griddle pan until really hot. Place the bread slices in the pan and turn after 1 minute to lightly char on both sides.

While the toast is still hot, rub each slice with the cut side of a clove garlic, then the cut side of a tomato, really squishing the seeds into the toasted surface.

Serve on a platter, drizzled with the olive oil, and sprinkled with salt and pepper.

Serves 4

anchovy & olive tapenade

see variations page 62

Olive tapenade is delicious, but the addition of anchovies and capers makes the famous spread multidimensional.

5–6 oz. pitted kalamata olives, drained
1 tbsp. capers, rinsed and drained
squeeze of fresh lemon juice

4 tbsp. really good olive oil
1/2 can anchovy fillets in oil, drained
freshly ground black pepper

Place all the ingredients in a food processor and puree to a coarse paste. Drizzle with a little extra olive oil and serve on bite-size toasts.

Serves 4

goat cheese on toast with figs

see variations page 63

Broiled goat cheese and figs on bread will not only become your tapas favorite, but will also make a super lunchtime snack.

4 ripe figs, quartered
4 slices rustic bread
2 tbsp. olive oil

7 oz. goat cheese
freshly ground black pepper

Preheat the broiler to high. Place the figs and bread under the broiler, drizzle with olive oil, and cook for 2 minutes until the upper side of the toast is golden.

Turn toasts over (the figs do not need to be turned) and place goat cheese on top. Grill for another 4 minutes until the goat cheese is browning but still holds its shape.

Place the toasts on a platter with the figs piled on top and sprinkled with black pepper. Serve immediately.

Serves 4

deep-fried stuffed olives

see variations page 64

Olives are one of the most common finger foods, but when stuffed, breaded, and deep-fried, they are as far from ordinary as possible.

7 oz. cream cheese, at room temperature
3 1/2 oz. (scant 1/2 cup) ricotta cheese,
    at room temperature
1 1/2 tsp. lemon zest
20 pitted large green olives, rinsed and dried
    thoroughly

3/4 cup fresh bread crumbs
3/4 cup all-purpose flour
1 egg
vegetable oil for deep-frying
sea salt, for serving

In a small bowl, combine the cheeses and lemon zest. Place the cheese mixture into a pastry bag. Pipe the mixture into each olive.

Put the bread crumbs in a food processor and blitz for about 1 minute until they have a very fine crumb texture.

Place the flour in a small bowl. Lightly beat the egg in another small bowl, and put the bread crumbs in a third small bowl. Dredge the olives in the flour. Using a slotted spoon, remove the olives and place them in the bowl with the beaten egg. Coat the olives with the egg and transfer them to the bowl of bread crumbs. Coat the olives with the crumbs.

Fill a deep skillet to half full with vegetable oil and heat to 375°F. Deep-fry the olives for 2–3 minutes, drain on paper towels, put into a serving dish, and sprinkle with sea salt.

Serves 4

duck rillettes with membrillo

see variations page 65

To make these rillettes (which are similar to a pâté), the duck is slowly cooked in its own fat and then shredded, mixed with some of the duck fat and juices, and allowed to set in a terrine. Normally served with cornichons, we have given these rillettes a Spanish twist and served them with some membrillo (quince paste) and plenty of hot toast.

6 duck legs, meat cut from the bones,
    skin reserved
sea salt and freshly ground black pepper
freshly grated nutmeg
1 tsp. ground cloves

1 bay leaf
fresh sage leaves
1 cup water
5 1/2 oz. membrillo, cut into 4 portions

Preheat the oven to 250°F. Place all the duck including the bones and skin, in a heavy lidded roasting pan with the salt, pepper, nutmeg, ground cloves, bay leaf, sage, and water. Set the pan in the bottom of the oven to cook for 3 hours until the fat has melted and the meat is falling apart.

Strain off the liquid fat and juices, saving them in a bowl. Discard the bones, any skin, and the bay leaf. Using forks, finely shred the meat. Check the seasoning, then lightly pack the meat into 4 ramekins or small lidded jars. Pour some of the reserved fat around the meat, making sure the top has a good layer of fat to seal it. Place in the refrigerator for 1 hour for the fat to set. Serve chilled, in the ramekins, with thinly sliced toasts and membrillo. They can be kept chilled in the refrigerator for up to 5 days.

Serves 4

mackerel tartare with horseradish

see variations page 66

Mackerel and horseradish are a match made in heaven, with the creaminess and heat balancing perfectly. Use a ready-made horseradish sauce if fresh horseradish is unavailable.

for the mackerel tartare
4 mackerel fillets, skinned and boned (around
    14 oz.)
2 tbsp. capers, finely chopped
2 small shallots, finely diced
4 tbsp. finely chopped fresh parsley
1 tsp. finely chopped fresh ginger
juice of 1 lemon
sea salt and freshly ground black pepper

for the creamy horseradish
4 tsp. grated fresh horseradish
1 tsp. sugar
1 tsp. salt
1/2 tsp. freshly ground black pepper
2 tsp. English mustard
1 tsp. malt vinegar
5 tbsp. whipping cream
rustic bread, sliced thin and toasted, for serving

Pick over the mackerel and remove any small bones with tweezers. Finely dice the fish (into about 1/4-inch pieces). Put in a bowl with the chopped capers, shallots, parsley, ginger, and lemon juice. Season with salt and pepper. Mix well, cover, and place in the refrigerator. The citrus juices will partially cure the fish, so allow 1/2 hour for this step. Don't leave it any longer, as the fish will "cook" too much.

Meanwhile, mix the horseradish well with the sugar, salt, pepper, mustard, and vinegar. Slowly beat in the cream, one tablespoon at a time, so that the mixture does not curdle. Serve the mackerel tartare with a dollop of the creamy horseradish and hot toasts.

Serves 4

manchego & serrano croquettas

see variations page 67

These croquettes are small nuggets of rich béchamel sauce that's been thickened and flavored, left to chill, and then breaded and fried. They are scrumptious little morsels.

1/2 cup (1 stick) butter
1/2 small onion, grated
1 cup flour
1/2 cup whole milk
1/2 tsp. freshly grated nutmeg
sea salt and freshly ground black pepper

2 oz. Serrano ham, cut into 1/4-inch cubes
3 oz. manchego cheese, finely grated
2 eggs, beaten with a splash of cold water
1 1/4 cups dried bread crumbs
vegetable oil for deep-frying

Melt butter over medium heat in a large pan. Gently fry the onion until soft. Stir in half the flour and cook another minute. Remove from heat and whisk in milk a little at a time until all the lumps are gone. Return to heat and cook, stirring frequently, until the sauce thickens. Add the nutmeg, salt, and pepper, followed by the ham and cheese. Remove from heat and transfer mixture to a shallow dish. Cover and refrigerate for 3 hours, until solid.

Place the beaten egg, bread crumbs, and remaining flour in three separate shallow bowls. With two spoons, form the croquette mixture into rounded balls about 1 1/4 inches in diameter. Dip each croquette in the flour, then cover in egg, then the bread crumbs. Make sure to cover the croquette thoroughly with all three layers so that the insides of the croquette don't seep out while cooking. Fill a heavy pan 2 1/2 inches deep with vegetable oil and heat to 375°F. Fry the croquettes in batches of about 3 at a time, turning over once, until golden on both sides; this should take about 3 minutes. Drain on paper towels and serve immediately, topped with a sprinkling of sea salt crystals.
Serves 4

croquettas with spinach

see variations page 68

Finding a crowd-pleasing vegetarian version of tapas can be quite a feat, but these oozy spinach croquettes are a winner with everyone.

1/2 cup (1 stick) butter
1 cup flour
1/2 cup whole milk
1/2 tsp. freshly grated nutmeg
1/2 tsp. cayenne pepper
sea salt and freshly ground black pepper

1 cup freshly grated Parmesan cheese
5 oz. fresh spinach, cooked, drained, and
    squeezed dry
2 eggs, beaten with a splash of cold water
1 1/4 cups dried bread crumbs
vegetable oil for frying

Melt butter over medium heat in a large pan. Stir in half the flour and cook another minute. Remove from heat and whisk in milk a little at a time until all the lumps are gone. Return to the heat and cook, stirring frequently, until the sauce is thick. Remove from the heat and add the nutmeg, cayenne pepper, salt, and pepper, followed by the Parmesan and cooked spinach. Place in a large dish, cover, and refrigerate for 3 hours, until set solid.

Place the beaten egg, bread crumbs, and remaining flour in three separate shallow bowls. With two spoons, form the croquette mixture into ovals by passing the sauce back and forth between the spoons in a rotating motion. Dip each croquette in the flour, then cover in egg, then the bread crumbs. Make sure to cover the croquettes thoroughly with all the layers so that the insides don't seep out while cooking.

Heat oil in a deep pan to 375°F. Fry the croquettes in batches of about 3 at a time, until golden; this should take about 3 minutes. Drain on paper towels and serve immediately. *Serves 4*

crispy eggs with wild mushrooms & truffle

see variations page 69

Wild mushrooms sautéed with garlic and white wine and finished with truffle oil. Sounds good, but topped with crisply fried quail eggs, it is divine.

4 tbsp. olive oil
4 quail eggs
4 tbsp. (1/2 stick) unsalted butter
1 small clove garlic, crushed
14 oz. mixed wild mushrooms, such as porcini, chanterelles, and matsutakes, cleaned

3 tbsp. medium-dry white wine
4 thick slices sourdough bread, toasted
drizzle of white truffle oil

In a heavy pan, heat the oil until very hot and the surface is just shimmering. Fry the quail eggs, being careful, as the hot fat will spit, for 1 1/2 minutes until the white is crisped underneath and the yolk is still runny. Place the eggs on paper towels to drain off excess oil.

Working quickly, melt the butter on high heat in a separate pan, but don't allow it to burn. Add the garlic and fry for 30 seconds, and then add all the mushrooms, keeping the heat up high so they cook in 2–3 minutes without wilting. For the last 30 seconds, add the wine, allowing it to largely evaporate away. Serve the mushrooms right away on a slice of toasted sourdough bread with a quail egg on top and a drizzle of truffle oil.

Serves 4

variations

puree de habas

see base recipe page 41

puree of chickpeas
Prepare the basic recipe, replacing the fava beans with cooked chickpeas
and adding the juice of 1/2 lemon.

puree of white beans
Prepare the basic recipe, replacing the fava beans with cooked
cannellini beans.

puree de habas with burrata
Prepare the basic recipe. Allow the puree to cool to room temperature
and serve on toasts with some ripe burrata cheese.

puree de habas with mint
Prepare the basic recipe, adding a small handful of fresh mint leaves
just before pureeing.

variations

pan con tomate

see base recipe page 43

bruschetta
Prepare the basic recipe, but instead of squishing the tomatoes into the bread, chop them up finely, mix with olive oil and a few leaves of fresh basil, and then serve on top of the toasts.

pan con tapenade
Prepare the basic recipe, omitting the tomatoes and spreading the toasts with 1 teaspoon tapenade (recipe page 44 or store-bought).

garlic bread
Prepare the basic recipe, omitting the tomatoes. Drizzle the toasts with extra olive oil.

roasted garlic bread
Prepare the basic recipe, omitting the tomatoes and raw garlic. Spread the toasts with 2–3 cloves from a head of roasted garlic.

variations

anchovy & olive tapenade

see base recipe page 44

anchovy & green olive tapenade
Prepare the basic recipe, replacing the kalamata olives with green olives.

simple olive tapenade
Prepare the basic recipe, omitting the capers and anchovies.

herby anchovy & olive tapenade
Prepare the basic recipe, adding 1 tablespoon each freshly chopped parsley, mint, and chervil before pureeing.

lemony anchovy & olive tapenade
Prepare the basic recipe, adding the zest and juice of 1 lemon.

goat cheese on toast with figs

see base recipe page 47

goat cheese on toast with figs & ham
Prepare the basic recipe, adding a slice of Serrano ham elegantly coiled on top of each toast.

goat cheese on toast with serrano ham
Prepare the basic recipe, omitting the broiled figs and adding a slice of Serrano ham coiled on top of each toast.

mozzarella cheese on toast with figs
Prepare the basic recipe, replacing the goat cheese with mozzarella cheese.

mozzarella cheese on toast with figs & serrano ham
Prepare the basic recipe, replacing the goat cheese with mozzarella cheese and adding a slice of Serrano ham coiled on top of each toast.

variations

deep-fried stuffed olives

see base recipe page 48

deep-fried stuffed olives with gorgonzola
Prepare the basic recipe, replacing the ricotta with Gorgonzola.

deep-fried stuffed olives with parmesan
Prepare the basic recipe, replacing the ricotta with Parmesan cheese.

deep-fried stuffed olives with herbs
Prepare the basic recipe, adding 1 tablespoon finely chopped mixed fresh herbs to the cheese mixture.

spicy deep-fried stuffed olives
Prepare the basic recipe, adding 1/2 teaspoon dried red pepper flakes to the cheese mixture.

variations

duck rillettes with membrillo

see base recipe page 51

classic duck rillettes
Prepare the basic recipe, replacing the membrillo with cornichons and small pickled onions.

duck rillettes with fresh herbs with membrillo
Prepare the basic recipe, adding 1 tablespoon chopped fresh tarragon and 1 tablespoon chopped fresh chervil to the shredded duck.

duck rillettes with capers with membrillo
Prepare the basic recipe, adding 1 tablespoon capers to the shredded duck.

pork rillettes with membrillo
Prepare the basic recipe, replacing the duck with about 1 pound pork belly, cooked the same way, skin-side down, for 4 hours.

variations

mackerel tartare with horseradish

see base recipe page 52

mackerel tartare with avocado
Prepare the basic recipe, but replace the creamy horseradish sauce with
1 very ripe avocado, mashed with the juice of 1/2 lime and sea salt.

salmon tartare with horseradish
Prepare the basic recipe, replacing the mackerel with fresh salmon fillet.

tuna tartare with avocado
Prepare the basic recipe, replacing the mackerel with fresh tuna fillet.
Replace the creamy horseradish sauce with 1 very ripe avocado, mashed
with the juice of 1/2 lime and sea salt.

sea bass tartare with dill & capers
Prepare the basic recipe, replacing the mackerel with fresh sea bass fillet.
Replace the creamy horseradish sauce with 1 teaspoon finely chopped fresh
dill mixed with 1 teaspoon chopped capers and the juice of 1/2 lemon.

manchego & serrano croquettas

see base recipe page 55

manchego croquettas
Prepare the basic recipe, but omit the ham.

serrano croquettas
Prepare the basic recipe, but omit the cheese.

manchego & shrimp croquettas
Prepare the basic recipe but omit the Serrano ham and replace with the same amount of small shrimp.

zamorano cheese & ground beef croquettas
Prepare the basic recipe, replacing the Serrano ham with the same amount of cooked ground beef and the manchego with zamorano cheese (a hard, sheep's milk cheese from Spain, which is nuttier and richer than manchego).

croquettas with spinach

see base recipe page 56

croquettas with spinach & truffle
Prepare the basic recipe, adding 1 teaspoon white truffle oil or paste to the filling.

croquettas with spinach & ham
Prepare the basic recipe, adding 2 ounces Serrano ham, finely chopped, with the spinach.

croquetta with four cheeses
Prepare the basic recipe, omitting the spinach and half the Parmesan.
Add 1/4 cup shredded manchego cheese, 1/2 cup shredded mozzarella, and 1/2 cup crumbled blue cheese to the mixture.

croquettas with four cheeses & truffle
Prepare the variation above, adding 1 teaspoon white truffle oil or paste to the mixture.

variations

crispy eggs with wild mushrooms & truffle

see base recipe page 59

crispy eggs with wild mushrooms
Prepare the basic recipe, but omit the truffle oil.

crispy eggs with wild mushrooms, parmesan & truffle
Prepare the basic recipe, adding 2 tablespoons freshly shaved Parmesan at
the end.

wild mushrooms & truffle on toast
Prepare the basic recipe, but omit the eggs.

crispy eggs with herby wild mushrooms & truffle
Prepare the basic recipe, adding 1 tablespoon chopped fresh parsley
and 1 teaspoon chopped fresh chervil during the last minute of cooking
the mushrooms.

pescado y mariscos

seafood tapas

What could be more Spanish than meaty gambas,

clams in spicy garlicky sauces, and tender squid.

Seafood tapas is a rousing riot of taste and texture.

fritto misto

see variations page 90

Fritto misto is a traditional tapas or appetizer comprised of a selection of deep-fried meats, fish, and vegetables. This recipe is a combination of deep-fried calamari, whitebait, and shrimp, with a interesting crunch of zucchini for good measure.

about 4 cups inexpensive olive oil
1/2 cup squid rings
1/2 cup whitebait or smelts
8 large raw shrimp, peeled, tail shells left on
1/2 tsp. sea salt

1/2 tsp. white pepper
3/4 cup flour
1 small zucchini, cut into thin rounds
2 lemons, cut into wedges, for serving

Preheat the oven to 300°F. Line a large baking pan with plenty of paper towels.

Pour the olive oil into a large saucepan or deep-fat fryer and heat to 375°F. To test the temperature, add a cube of bread to the pan. At 375°F, it will brown in 30 seconds.

Season the seafood lightly with salt. Mix together the salt, pepper, and flour. Toss the seafood and zucchini, a few pieces at a time, in the seasoned flour and deep-fry, in batches, for 1 minute until crisp and lightly golden. Use a slotted spoon to lift onto the paper-lined pan to drain. Keep warm in the oven while you cook the rest. Serve hot with the lemon wedges.

Serves 4

gambas pil pil

see variations page 91

This popular way of serving shrimp in Spain should arrive at the table *pil-pileando*, which means the fragrant scarlet oil should be bubbling and spluttering as the dish is set down. If you can't find king prawns, royal red shrimp are a good substitute.

12 raw medium king prawns, peeled and
   deveined
1 tsp. sea salt
1/3 cup extra-virgin olive oil

2 cloves garlic, thinly sliced
1 1-inch piece dried red chile, seeded
small pinch paprika
1 tbsp. chopped fresh parsley

Place the prawns in a bowl, sprinkle with the salt, and toss. Let stand 15 minutes and then pat dry.

Heat the oil in a medium-sized pan over high heat. Add the garlic and dried chile and stir. When the garlic becomes golden, add the prawns and stir until just cooked through, about 2 minutes. Stir in the paprika and parsley for the last 30 seconds of cooking. Transfer to a serving dish with the oil and serve with bread to dunk.

Serves 4

salt cod fritters with saffron aïoli

see variations page 92

Salted cod has been produced in countries around the Atlantic for over 500 years. Once soaked and rehydrated, it has a delightfully subtle and surprisingly unsalty flavor. These days, with fishing stocks declining, cod is often replaced by more sustainable fish such as pollock.

for the aïoli
2 organic free-range egg yolks
pinch salt
3 cloves garlic, peeled and crushed
juice of 1 lemon
1 cup extra-virgin olive oil
1/2 cup canola oil
20 strands saffron, soaked in 1 tbsp. boiling
  water

for the fritters
9 oz. salt cod
1 cup mashed floury potatoes (such as russet)
4 tbsp. milk or cream
3 scallions, finely chopped
2 tbsp. chopped fresh parsley
3 free-range eggs, separated
salt and freshly ground black pepper
vegetable oil for frying

To make the saffron aioli, place the 2 egg yolks in a bowl and add salt, garlic, and lemon juice. Whisk to combine. Dribble in the oil, as slowly as you possibly can, whisking continuously (an electric mixer makes this much easier). Continue to whisk until both oils are incorporated. You should end up with a thick, unctuous, garlicky mayonnaise. Stir in the soaked saffron, including the water that the strands were steeped in. This can be kept, covered, in the refrigerator for up to 2 days.

Soak the salt cod in cold water in the refrigerator 12–24 hours in advance, changing the water halfway through. Drain the water, rinse the salt cod, then place it in a pan, cover with fresh water, and bring to a boil. Turn off the heat and leave for 5 minutes. Remove the fish

from the pan. Peel off the skin and flake the fish, removing any tiny bones. Add the mashed potatoes, milk, scallions, parsley, egg yolks, and salt to taste. Mix well. Whisk the egg whites to soft peaks and fold into the mixture. Heat a saucepan a third full of oil until a bit of bread sizzles and browns in a minute. Add the salt cod mixture in tablespoonfuls and fry until brown all over. Drain for 2 minutes on paper towels, then serve with the aïoli on the side.

Serves 4

king prawns with garlic & smoked paprika

see variations page 93

This recipe encapsulates the simplicity of rustic Spanish cooking. The mingling flavors of the marinade combine beautifully with the sweet succulent prawns, while charred edges from the barbecue or griddle give the slightest of crunches and a heady smoked aroma. You can substitute jumbo shrimp, but the king prawns or royal red shrimp look much more authentic.

4 king prawns, heads off, deveined,
    but shells on
1 tsp. sea salt
3 cloves garlic, finely chopped

1/2 tsp. smoked paprika
2 tbsp. olive oil
zest and juice of 1 lemon

Place the prawns in a bowl with the salt, garlic, paprika, olive oil, and lemon zest. Mix, then let marinate for 15 minutes.

Heat a griddle pan or barbecue grill on high until it begins to smoke. Lay the prawns on the pan or grill and cook for 2–3 minutes on each side until charred on the outside but nice and opaque in the middle. Sprinkle with the lemon juice in the last minute of cooking. Transfer to a serving dish and eat with your fingers.

Serves 4

griddled sardines & rosemary salt

see variations page 94

Rosemary and oily fish are a marriage made in heaven! Make sure you get your fish merchant to butterfly the sardines, which means the center bone is removed, leaving a boneless piece of fish. As a result, these lovely crisp little fishes can be served whole on rustic toast to be eaten with ease and pleasure.

2 sprigs fresh rosemary
1 tsp. sea salt
4 slices sourdough bread

extra-virgin olive oil
8 fresh sardines, butterflied

Remove the leaves from the rosemary sprigs and chop them very finely. Mix with the salt and then pound in a mortar and pestle until the salt turns a little green from the rosemary oil. Set aside.

Heat a dry griddle pan on high heat until it is smoking. Griddle the slices of bread until slightly charred on both sides. Lay the slices on 4 plates and drizzle each one with a little oil. Season the sardines with half the rosemary salt, then add them to the dry griddle, skin-side down, and cook for 1–2 minutes per side. Remove and lay 2 sardines on each piece of bread and sprinkle with the rest of the rosemary salt to serve.

Serves 4

griddled calamari with garlic, orange & smoked paprika

see variations page 95

It is important in this recipe that the pan is exceptionally hot so the squid is quickly cooked to tender perfection. Squid must always be cooked very fast over high heat or slowly over a long period, otherwise the result is a chewy, rubberlike disaster.

1 large squid (about 1/2 lb.), membrane and
    sac removed
1/2 tsp. sea salt
3 cloves garlic, finely chopped

zest of 1 orange
1/2 tsp. hot smoked paprika
2 tbsp. olive oil

Open up the squid by cutting along the side seam. Wash and dry thoroughly. Very gently, with the tip of a sharp knife, score the squid in a crisscross pattern. Cut into 4 pieces. Place the squid in a bowl with the salt, garlic, orange zest, paprika, and olive oil. Let marinate for 5 minutes.

Heat a griddle over a high heat until it is smoking, and then lay the pieces of squid on the griddle. (I like to weight them down to stop them from curling up, using something heavy like another pan.) Cook for 1–2 minutes on each side. Cut into 2 1/2-inch diamonds and place on a serving plate.

Serves 4

clams with chorizo, garlic & chile

see variations page 96

Clams and Spanish chorizo make an exceptionally good combination. The smoky meatiness of the sausage brings an interesting dimension to the seafood. I recommend serving this in a big tapas dish, with a few chunks of crusty bread to mop up the delicious spicy juices at the end.

1/2 lb. small clams (I like cherrystone clams)
1 tbsp. extra-virgin olive oil
1 (3-oz.) piece semidry Spanish chorizo,
    chopped into small cubes

2 cloves garlic, finely chopped
1 red chile, finely chopped

Scrub the clams in cold water and dispose of any broken ones. Heat the oil in a lidded pan. Add the chorizo and fry for 3 minutes or until the chorizo starts to turn golden. Add the garlic and chile, and then the washed clams. Cook for about 3 minutes with the lid on. When all the clams are open, serve immediately in a tapas dish.

Serves 4

scallops with blood sausages & sage

see variations page 97

This unusual dish of sweet scallops accompanied by the deep iron flavor of morcilla (Spanish blood sausage) and crisped sage leaves is quite spectacular.

1 tbsp. (1/8 stick) butter
a few leaves of fresh sage
4 large diver scallops

2 (3–oz.) Spanish blood sausages (such as morcilla), each cut into 4 pieces

Place a pan over high heat and add the butter. When it starts to foam, add the sage leaves and scallops. Let the scallops caramelize, so don't move them for 1–2 minutes, then flip them over and cook on the other side. If the sage starts to scorch before the scallops have cooked, remove from the pan. Remove the scallops once they have turned golden and are caramelized on both sides but are still opaque in the center.

When the scallops have been removed, add the sausages to the pan. Fry for 1–2 minutes or until they have blackened and crisped on the outside but are still soft in the center. Serve the scallops, sausages, and sage together in a serving dish.

Serves 4

paella with seafood & chicken

see variations page 98

The most iconic of Spanish dishes, the joy of paella comes from flinging in whatever big-flavored ingredients you fancy, so feel free to experiment.

1/4 cup good olive oil
6 oz. chorizo, cut into thin slices
2 cloves garlic, finely chopped
1 large onion, finely diced
1 red bell pepper, diced
2 large tomatoes, seeded and diced
pinch dried red pepper flakes
1 cup paella rice (such as Goya brand)
1 tsp. smoked paprika
1/2 cup dry white wine

2 cups chicken stock heated with 1/4 tsp. saffron strands
sea salt and freshly ground black pepper
8 chicken thighs, each chopped in half
8 raw small clams, cleaned
1/3 cup frozen peas
1 head garlic, cloves separated and peeled
6 raw jumbo shrimp in shells
2 cups (1 lb.) raw squid, cleaned and sliced
1 tbsp. chopped fresh flat-leaf parsley

Heat half the olive oil in a paella dish or heavy saucepan. Add the chorizo and fry until crisp. Add the garlic, onion, and pepper, and heat until softened. Add the tomatoes, red pepper flakes, and rice. Stir until all the grains of rice are nicely coated and glossy. Add the paprika and wine, and when it is bubbling, pour in the hot chicken stock and season with salt and pepper. In a separate skillet, heat a tablespoon of oil and brown the chicken thighs, then add them to the paella dish and cook for 5–10 minutes. Place the clams in the dish with the joint facing down so that the edges open outward. Sprinkle in the peas and continue to cook gently, uncovered, for another 10 minutes. Meanwhile, heat the remaining oil with the garlic cloves in a separate pan. Add the shrimp. Fry quickly for 1–2 minutes, then add them to the paella. Repeat with the squid and add them to the paella. Scatter the chopped parsley over the paella and serve immediately.

Serves 4

black paella with garlic squid

see variations page 99

If you have not used it before, do not be put off by the squid ink. It is a very familiar ingredient in coastal Mediterranean cooking, where it is prized for its subtle iron flavor.

2 tbsp. olive oil
4 scallions, trimmed and finely chopped
3 cloves garlic, finely chopped
1 red chile, finely chopped
1 cup diced cleaned squid plus 2 small squid, cleaned for garnish
1 cup paella rice (such as Goya brand)
3/4 cup white wine

2 1/2 cups fish stock
2 tsp. light olive oil
1 clove garlic, finely chopped
1 Brussels sprout, leaves only (optional)
5 tbsp. squid ink
1 tbsp. butter
sea salt and freshly ground black pepper
2 tbsp. chopped fresh parsley

Over moderate heat, heat 1 tablespoon oil in a heavy skillet. Fry the scallions, garlic, and chile for 1 minute. Add 1 cup diced cleaned squid and fry until lightly colored and the pan is dry. Remove everything from the pan and set aside. Heat the remaining oil in the pan, add the rice, and fry for 2–3 minutes. Pour in the white wine and bring to a boil. Pour in the fish stock and cook, uncovered, for 15 minutes or until the rice is nearly cooked. Meanwhile, for the garlic squid garnish, slice the small squid into rings, keeping the tentacles whole. Heat the olive oil and garlic in a skillet over medium heat, add the squid, and pan-fry for a few minutes until golden brown. For the last minute, add the Brussels sprout leaves. Sprinkle in the chopped parsley and set aside. Stir the reserved squid and scallion mixture into the rice. Add the squid ink with a little more stock if necessary. Stir well. At this stage the rice should be perfectly cooked and should take on the dark black color of the ink. Stir in the butter and season with salt and pepper. Serve the squid garnish on top of the blackened paella.

Serves 4

variations

fritto misto

see base recipe page 71

fritto misto with sweet potato
Prepare the basic recipe, replacing the zucchini with 1/2 cup sweet potato in 1/4-inch-thick rounds and adding 1/2 teaspoon cayenne pepper and 1/2 teaspoon paprika to the seasoned flour.

spicy fritto misto
Prepare the basic recipe, adding 1/2 teaspoon ground cumin and 1/2 teaspoon ground coriander to the seasoned flour.

fritto misto with scallops
Prepare the basic recipe, replacing the whitebait with 1/2 cup small scallops and adding the grated zest of 1 lemon to the seasoned flour.

deep-fried vegetables
Prepare the basic recipe, replacing all the seafood with 2 thickly sliced onions and 2 parsnips and 2 carrots, each peeled and cut into batons.

variations

gambas pil pil

see base recipe page 73

chicken pil pil
Prepare the basic recipe, replacing the prawns with 1 boneless and skinless
chicken breast beaten flat and cut into strips.

monkfish pil pil
Prepare the basic recipe, replacing the prawns with 1 cup cubed monkfish.

spicy pil pil
Prepare the basic recipe, adding 1/2 teaspoon ground cumin and 1/2 teaspoon
ground coriander to the pan with the garlic and chile.

gambas pil pil with ginger
Prepare the basic recipe, adding 1 teaspoon grated fresh ginger to the pan with
the garlic and chile. Omit the paprika.

salt cod fritters with saffron aïoli

see base recipe page 74

shrimp fritters with saffron aïoli
Prepare the basic recipe, replacing the salt cod with 1 cup chopped raw shrimp, mixed into the potato mixture.

salt cod fritters with aïoli
Prepare the basic recipe, omitting the saffron and boiling water in the aioli, so it's a basic garlic aïoli.

salt cod fritters with sweet garlic aïoli
Prepare the basic recipe, replacing the saffron and boiling water with 1 tablespoon sweet chili sauce to make a sweet garlic aïoli.

salt cod fritters with smoky aïoli
Prepare the basic recipe, replacing the saffron with 1 tablespoon chipotle chiles in adobo sauce, to make a smoky aïoli.

king prawns with garlic & smoked paprika

see base recipe page 77

king prawns with garlic, cilantro, lemongrass & lemon
Prepare the basic recipe, replacing the paprika in the marinade with
1 tablespoon chopped fresh cilantro and a 1-inch piece of lemongrass,
chopped finely.

king prawns with garlic & peppercorns
Prepare the basic recipe, replacing the paprika and lemon zest in the marinade
with 1 1/2 teaspoons crushed pink peppercorns (available in jars from your
supermarket).

king prawns with garlic, smoked paprika, lemon & chile
Prepare the basic recipe, adding 1 chopped small red chile to the marinade.

king prawns with garlic, ginger, chile & cilantro
Prepare the basic recipe, replacing the paprika and lemon zest in the marinade
with 1 teaspoon grated fresh ginger, 1 chopped green chile, and 1 tablespoon
chopped fresh cilantro.

variations

griddled sardines & rosemary salt

see base recipe page 78

griddled sardines & fennel & salt

Prepare the basic recipe, omitting the rosemary. Place fennel fronds in the center of each of the butterflied sardines, then fold the sardine back into its natural shape before cooking. Use the salt to season the fish naturally.

griddled mullet & rosemary salt

Prepare the basic recipe, replacing the sardines with small filleted red mullet (2 fillets per fish). Your fish merchant will fillet them for you.

griddled sardines & rosemary salt & polenta

Prepare the basic recipe, replacing the sourdough bread with 4 slices of griddled polenta. Polenta can be bought as a solid block in most supermarkets, which makes slicing easy.

griddled mackerel & rosemary salt

Prepare the basic recipe, replacing the sardines with mackerel filleted by your fish merchant. Rub well with the rosemary salt.

griddled calamari with garlic, orange & smoked paprika

see base recipe page 81

spicy griddled calamari with garlic & lemongrass

Prepare the basic recipe, replacing the orange zest and paprika in the marinade with 1/2 teaspoon dried red pepper flakes and a 1/2-inch piece of lemongrass, finely chopped.

griddled monkfish with garlic, orange & smoked paprika

Prepare the basic recipe, replacing the squid with 3/4 cup monkfish in 1/2-inch-thick slices.

spicy griddled calamari with garlic, lemon & mint

Prepare the basic recipe, replacing the orange zest and smoked paprika in the marinade with lemon zest, 1 tablespoon chopped red chiles, 1 finely chopped scallion, and 1 tablespoon chopped fresh mint.

griddled calamari with garlic & lemon thyme

Prepare the basic recipe, replacing the orange zest and paprika in the marinade with 1 teaspoon chopped fresh lemon thyme. Squeeze the juice of half a lemon over the cooked squid before serving.

variations

clams with chorizo, garlic & chile

see base recipe page 82

clams with chorizo, garlic, chile & thyme
Prepare the basic recipe, adding a pinch of chopped fresh thyme with the garlic and chile. Fry gently for 1 minute before adding the clams.

clams with chorizo, garlic & chile in wine sauce
Prepare the basic recipe, adding 1 chopped shallot to the olive oil and sautéing until it is transparent. Then add a generous 1/2 cup white wine and 1 tablespoon chopped fresh parsley. Cook until the wine is reduced in half, and then add the garlic and chorizo and clams.

clams with chorizo, garlic, chile & tomatoes
Prepare the basic recipe, adding 3 chopped fresh tomatoes 1 minute after the garlic and chile. Cook for an additional 3 minutes before adding the clams.

clams with chorizo, garlic, chile & roasted peppers
Prepare the basic recipe, adding 2 tablespoons chopped roasted peppers at the same time as the garlic and chile. Cook for an additional 3 minutes before adding the clams.

scallops with blood sausages & sage

see base recipe page 85

scallops with chorizo & sage
Prepare the basic recipe, replacing the sausages with coarsely chopped chorizo.
Serve the chorizo as a bed with the scallops placed on top.

piquant caramelized scallops
Prepare the basic recipe, omitting the blood sausages and sage. Prepare a rub
for the scallops with 1/4 teaspoon cayenne pepper, 1/4 teaspoon ground
turmeric, and 1/4 teaspoon ground coriander. Rub the mixture over the
scallops and leave for 10 minutes to absorb the flavors. Cook the rubbed
scallops in the butter as in the basic recipe.

scallops with garlic sausages & sage
Prepare the basic recipe, replacing the blood sausages with cubed Polish garlic
sausage. Pork is an excellent accompaniment to scallops.

scallops with pancetta & sage
Prepare the basic recipe, replacing the blood sausages with pancetta pieces.

variations

paella with seafood & chicken

see base recipe page 86

paella with seafood & rabbit
Prepare the basic recipe, replacing the chicken thighs with rabbit, cut into
pieces the size of a chicken thigh.

vegetarian paella
Prepare the basic recipe, using just 1/8 cup olive oil and 2 sliced cloves
garlic, and replacing the chicken, seafood, and chorizo with 1 each of red,
green, and yellow bell peppers, cut into cubes; 1 cup cubed butternut
squash; and 1 1/3 cups sliced mushrooms. Use vegetable stock instead of
chicken stock. Roast the cubed vegetables in the oil with the garlic for
15 minutes and add to the paella at the very end.

paella with seafood, lobster & chicken
Prepare the basic recipe, adding 1 cooked lobster tail, cut into large pieces,
to the paella when you add the shrimp.

paella with seafood
Prepare the basic recipe, omitting the chicken.

black paella with garlic squid

see base recipe page 89

black paella
Prepare the basic recipe, omit the squid topping and the Brussel sprout leaves for a smoother paella. The delicate taste of the squid ink will be wonderful on its own.

tomato paella with garlic squid
Prepare the basic recipe, replacing the squid ink with 1 (14-ounce) can chopped tomatoes.

black paella with seafood with garlic squid
Prepare the basic recipe, adding 8 shrimp, 12 mussels, and 12 large clams about 7 minutes before the rice is cooked. Stir well. The shellfish is cooked when all the shells are opened; discard any whose shells do not open.

seafood paella with garlic squid
Prepare the basic recipe, omitting the squid ink.

pollo y pato
poultry tapas

Chicken's subtle flavor make it a perfect partner for the big punchy tastes of tapas. From wing to breast to thighs, almost the entire bird is used to create a selection of cunningly elegant delights.

pollo a la ajillo

see variations page 117

This simple recipe, translated as "chicken fried with garlic," is a staple on any traditional tapas menu. Do not allow the garlic to overcook and become too brown as the flavor will turn unpleasantly bitter.

4 boneless and skinless chicken thighs
sea salt and freshly ground black pepper
2 tbsp. flour
3 tbsp. extra-virgin olive oil

4 large cloves garlic, thinly sliced
1/2 cup good-quality dry sherry (such as fino)
1 tbsp. brandy
1 tbsp. chopped fresh flat-leaf parsley

Cut the thighs into 4 pieces each. Season with salt and pepper and then coat with flour. In a skillet, heat the oil and add the garlic. Gently fry until the garlic begins to turn golden, then remove and set aside. Add the chicken to the pan. Fry for 3 minutes on each side or until cooked through. Return the garlic to the pan.

Pour in the sherry and brandy. Flambé if you're feeling brave, or just let the alcohol bubble away until only about 1–2 tablespoons are left in the pan. Stir in the parsley and season with salt and pepper. Transfer to a serving dish.

Serves 4

griddled chicken thighs with harissa, lime & garlic

see variations page 118

Harissa is a piquant spice mix particularly popular in Moroccan cooking. Rose harissa is a similar spice blend with the addition of rose petals, which gives it an appealing aromatic depth. These flavors work beautifully as a rub on any meat but give a particular interest to the subtleties of chicken.

4 chicken thighs, boneless, with skin
1 tbsp. harissa (rose harissa is my favorite)
1 tbsp. olive oil
2 cloves garlic, finely chopped

zest and juice of 1 lime
sea salt and freshly ground black pepper
lime wedges to serve

Place the chicken thighs in a bowl. Add the harissa, oil, garlic, lime zest, salt, and pepper. Let marinate for 1 hour.

Heat a griddle on high heat until it begins to smoke. Lay the chicken thighs, skin side down, on the griddle. Cook for 3 minutes on each side or until lightly charred and cooked through. For the last minute, sprinkle with the lime juice. Transfer to a serving dish and serve sprinkled with more sea salt and lime wedges.

Serves 4

chicken cordon bleu goujons

see variations page 119

Cordon bleu is a gastronomic term meaning of the highest class. Therefore, this moist chicken wrapped in ham with oozy cheese is just about as delicious as you can get. To make sure this recipe has a real Spanish flair, it uses the quintessentially Spanish ingredients of manchego cheese and Serrano ham.

1 skinless and boneless chicken breast
1 6-inch-long, 1/8-inch-thick slice manchego
   cheese
1–2 slices Serrano ham
1/2 cup all-purpose flour, seasoned with salt
   and pepper

1 egg, whisked
1 1/2 cups fresh bread crumbs
1/4 cup olive oil

Place the chicken breast between pieces of waxed paper. With either a meat mallet or a rolling pin, flatten the meat, like a schnitzel. Lay the cheese on top and then the slices of ham on top of the cheese. Tuck the ham around slightly to encase the cheese.

Set out the flour, egg, and bread crumbs in different bowls. First coat the chicken in flour, then egg, and then bread crumbs. The cheese needs to be totally encased, so you may need to repeat the last steps to be sure.

Heat the oil in a skillet, add the breaded chicken, and pan-fry for 3–4 minutes on each side or until golden, crisp, and cooked through. Drain on paper towels and then carve into fingers. Place in a serving dish and serve immediately.

Serves 4

roast chicken with truffle gnocchi, sage butter & cavolo nero

see variations page 120

Making your own gnocchi might seem a little daunting, but I assure you, once you have eaten fresh gnocchi, you will never go back to store-bought.

1 tbsp. olive oil
1 chicken breast, with skin on and wing tip in
sea salt and black pepper
1/4 cup shredded cavolo nero (black kale)
for the gnocchi
4 medium floury potatoes (such as russet),
    baked and still hot
1/2 cup Italian "00" (or all-purpose) flour, plus
    extra for dusting

1/4 tsp. fine sea salt
2 1/2 tbsp. finely grated Parmesan cheese,
    plus extra for serving
1/2 tsp. white truffle paste
1 egg yolk, lightly beaten
for the sage & truffle butter
2 tbsp. (1/4 stick) unsalted butter
4 large fresh sage leaves
1 tsp. truffle-infused olive oil

Preheat the oven to 400°F. Heat an ovenproof skillet over medium-high heat and add the oil. Season the chicken with salt and pepper, then lay it skin-side down in the skillet and fry for 2–3 minutes until the skin is crisp and golden. Turn it over, then place in oven for 8–10 minutes or until cooked through. Remove and let rest, covered, to keep warm.

To make the gnocchi, scoop out the flesh of the baked potatoes. Mash potato in a large mixing bowl. Form a well in the center and add the flour, salt, and Parmesan. Stir, and mix in the truffle paste and beaten egg yolk. With clean, floured hands, press the mixture together to form a dough, adding a little more flour if the mixture is too wet. Do not overwork. Put the dough on a floured surface and shape into a long log. Cut into 1-inch lengths and press

down the tops with a fork, then gently press the sides to resemble pillows. Cover with plastic wrap so the gnocchi does not dry out while you make the sauce.

Meanwhile, put the butter and sage in a small pan over medium heat. Let the butter cook until it is golden brown and smelling nutty. Remove from the heat and stir in the truffle oil. Keep warm. Bring a large pan of salted water to a boil. Poach the gnocchi and kale for 1–2 minutes or until the gnocchi has risen to the surface. Drain, then add to the sage and truffle oil butter sauce. Return the pan to medium-high heat and toss until the gnocchi is well coated and browning in some spots. Transfer to a serving dish. Carve the chicken and arrange pieces on top of the gnocchi. Drizzle with the chicken juices and any remaining butter sauce.

Serves 4

chicken cutlet with serrano ham & marsala

see variations page 121

Serrano ham or "mountain ham" is a typical dry-cured Spanish ham. This means it is generally served raw in thin slices, but when cooked it crisps up beautifully, creating a rich salty flavor that complements the chicken, zingy lemon, and herbs.

1 skinless and boneless chicken breast
sea salt and freshly ground black pepper
1–2 slices Serrano ham
2 fresh sage leaves
1 lemon slice

1 tbsp. flour
1 tbsp. olive oil
1/2 tsp. butter
1/2 cup dry Marsala wine

Put the chicken breast between pieces of waxed paper and, using a meat mallet or rolling pin, flatten to a thickness of about 1/4 inch. Season with salt and pepper.

Lay a slice of ham on top of the chicken and put a sage leaf on top. Cover the sage with a slice of lemon and secure the whole thing with a toothpick. Lightly dust with flour on both sides. Heat the oil and butter in a skillet. Cook the chicken for about 3 minutes on each side until golden brown and cooked through. Add the Marsala to the pan and quickly bubble down until thickened and reduced by about half. Transfer the chicken to a serving dish and pour the sauce on top.

Serves 4

chicken with potatoes, olives & sherry

see variations page 122

This quick sticky stew is a hearty, rustic, and homey dish that is really satisfying when you want something light but comforting. The grating of the orange zest at the end gives an interesting twist to the flavor.

4 boneless and skinless chicken thighs
sea salt and freshly ground black pepper
2 tbsp. flour
4 tbsp. extra-virgin olive oil
4 large cloves garlic, thinly sliced
8 green olives

2 small waxy potatoes (such as Yukon Gold),
    cooked and quartered
1/2 cup good-quality dry sherry (such as fino)
1 tbsp. brandy
1 tbsp. chopped fresh flat-leaf parsley
zest of 1/2 orange

Cut each chicken thigh into 4 pieces. Season with salt and pepper, and then coat with flour. In a skillet, heat the oil and add the garlic. Gently fry until the garlic starts to turn golden. Remove and set aside, then add the chicken. Fry for 3 minutes on each side or until cooked through. Return the garlic to the pan, and add the olives and potatoes.

Pour in the sherry and brandy, flambé if you're feeling brave, but otherwise let the alcohol bubble away until only about 1–2 tablespoons are left in the pan. Stir in the parsley and orange zest, and season with salt and pepper. Transfer to a serving dish.

Serves 4

chicken wings with honey & paprika

see variations page 123

A favorite tapas dish of really simple finger food. The paprika and honey marinade gives the chicken an irresistible sticky, spicy glaze.

8 chicken wings, well washed
2 cloves garlic, chopped
1 tsp. paprika
1/2 tsp. sea salt

1/2 tsp. freshly ground black pepper
1 tsp. finely grated lemon zest
3 tbsp. honey

Cut wings into portions through the joints, discarding wingtips. Combine the remaining ingredients in a bowl. Add wings and turn over to coat in the mixture. Cover and refrigerate for 2–3 hours or overnight, stirring occasionally.

Heat oven to 400°F. Spread wings over the bottom of a baking dish and brush liberally with marinade. Roast for 30–35 minutes, until golden brown. Turn the wings halfway through the baking. Transfer to a serving dish.

Serves 4

duck breast with quince sauce

see variations page 124

The delicate and perfumed flavor of quince is a great match for earthy duck.
Cooking the fruit in this selection of spices gives a subtle, exciting twist to the sauce.

1 1/4 cups dry or sweet white wine
1 quince, peeled and cut in small chunks
1 tbsp. sherry vinegar
1 tbsp. brown sugar
pinch ground cinnamon

pinch ground mace
1 star anise
2 whole cloves
1 duck breast
2 tbsp. (1/4 stick) butter, cubed

Pour the wine into a saucepan and add the quince, vinegar, sugar, and spices. Bring to a boil,
and continue gently boiling for about 5 minutes. Remove from heat, cover, and let cool while
you cook the duck. Score the duck breast skin and remove the fat. Place skin-side down in a
dry skillet and cook gently over a low heat, for roughly 8 minutes, then turn over and cook
for another 3–4 minutes. At this point the duck should be cooked to medium doneness.
Remove from the heat and rest while you complete the dish.

Discard the rendered duck fat from the pan, add 1/3 cup of the quince cooking sauce and
the quince chunks, and cook down, turning the quince as you go, and reduce until you are
left with a strong sauce. Whisk in a few cubes of cold butter, cube by cube, until the sauce is
velvety and thick.

Cut the duck breast into strips and serve on a warm plate with pieces of quince and some
sauce poured on top.

Serves 4

duck, beet & pickled walnut salad

see variations page 125

This unusual salad is made especially striking due to the quantity of strong but complementary flavors involved. Pickled walnuts, a treat often found at Christmastime, go perfectly with meaty duck and sweet beets.

for the dressing
2 tbsp. walnut oil
2 tsp. red wine vinegar
sea salt and freshly ground black pepper
for the salad
1 duck breast
sea salt and freshly ground black pepper
4 pickled walnuts, cut into quarters

1 cup watercress, large stems removed
1 scallion, thinly sliced
1 head Belgian endive, separated into leaves, the core sliced
1 small orange, peeled and segmented
1 1/2 cups cooked beets (canned beets are fine), cut into wedges

Combine the dressing ingredients and set aside. Heat a large nonstick skillet over medium heat. Season the duck and place it in the pan, skin-side down, and fry for 8 minutes. (During this time a large amount of fat will come from the skin and the skin will turn golden, but the flesh shouldn't cook too much.) Turn the duck over and cook for about 3–4 minutes on the other side. The duck should be cooked to medium doneness. Remove the duck from the pan and set aside to rest.

Add the walnuts and dressing to the pan and turn off the heat. The dressing should bubble and reduce a little in the remaining heat. Put the watercress, scallion, and endive in a bowl, and coat with half the dressing. Pile onto a plate with the oranges and beets, then scatter with the walnuts. Slice the duck, arrange on top of the salad, and drizzle with the remaining dressing and any juices from the duck.

Serves 4

pollo a la ajillo

see base recipe page 101

conejo a la ajillo
Prepare the basic recipe, replacing chicken thighs with rabbit portions. Cook the rabbit a couple of minutes longer on each side to cook through.

pollo a la ajillo with port
Prepare the basic recipe, replacing the dry sherry with a port, especially a white port, to give a greater depth of flavor.

calvados pollo a la ajillo
Prepare the basic recipe, replacing the sherry and brandy with 1/2 cup Calvados. Add a couple tablespoons of cream. Replace parsley with 1/2 tablespoon fresh tarragon leaves.

pollo a la ajillo with thyme
Prepare the basic recipe, replacing the parsley with 1/2 tablespoon chopped fresh thyme.

griddled chicken thighs with harissa, lime & garlic

see base recipe page 103

chile chicken thighs
Prepare the basic recipe, replacing the harissa with 1 teaspoon dried red pepper flakes and 1 teaspoon smoked paprika. Omit the lime zest and juice.

chicken thighs with a thai rub
Prepare the basic recipe, replacing the harissa with a paste made from a 1/2-inch piece of fresh ginger, grated; a 1-inch piece of lemongrass; and 1/2 green chile.

herby chicken thighs with lime & garlic
Prepare the basic recipe, replacing the harissa with 1/2 tablespoon chopped fresh rosemary, 1/2 teaspoon chopped fresh thyme, and 1/4 teaspoon chopped fresh mint.

harissa lamb cutlets
Prepare the basic recipe, replacing chicken thighs with lamb cutlets. Be careful not to overcook them, and let them rest for a few minutes before serving.

variations

chicken cordon bleu goujons

see base recipe page 104

veal cordon bleu goujons
Prepare the basic recipe, replacing the chicken with veal escalopes.

honey-smoked ham goujons
Prepare the basic recipe, replacing the Serrano ham with some
honey-smoked ham.

pork & goat cheese goujons
Prepare the basic recipe, replacing the chicken with thin slices of boneless pork
and the manchego cheese with a Spanish goat cheese, such as Ibores.

matzo-crusted chicken cordon bleu goujons
Prepare the basic recipe, replacing the bread crumbs with crushed matzos for a
lighter crumb crust.

roast chicken with truffle gnocchi, sage butter & cavolo nero

see base recipe page 106

roast chicken with basil gnocchi, sage butter & cavolo nero
Prepare the basic recipe, replacing the truffle paste in the gnocchi
with 1 tablespoon finely chopped fresh basil. Omit the truffle oil in the
sage butter.

roast chicken with olive gnocchi, sage butter & cavolo nero
Prepare the basic recipe, replacing the truffle paste in the gnocchi with
1 tablespoon olive paste. Omit the truffle oil in the sage butter.

roast chicken with truffle gnocchi, sage butter & savoy cabbage
Prepare the basic recipe, replacing the kale with finely sliced Savoy cabbage.

roast chicken with spinach gnocchi, sage butter & cavolo nero
Prepare the basic recipe, adding 1/2 cup cooked, drained, and squeezed-dry
fresh spinach to the gnocchi.

chicken cutlet with serrano ham & marsala

see base recipe page 108

veal cutlet with serrano ham & marsala
Prepare the basic recipe, replacing the chicken breast with veal.

chicken cutlet with serrano ham & vermouth
Prepare the basic recipe, replacing the Marsala with white vermouth.

chicken cutlet with bacon & marsala
Prepare the basic recipe, replacing the ham with finely sliced smoked bacon or pancetta for a more smoky flavor.

chicken cutlet with serrano ham & zingy orange sauce
Prepare the basic recipe, replacing the Marsala with freshly squeezed orange juice and the zest of 1/2 orange.

chicken with potatoes, olives & sherry

see base recipe page 111

beef with potatoes, olives & sherry

Prepare the basic recipe, replacing the chicken with the same quantity
of beef fillet, cut into 1/4-inch slices. Omit the seasoned flour. After cooking
the garlic in the oil, raise the heat of the skillet and cook the steak for
2 minutes per side. Remove the steak from the pan to rest while you
continue cooking.

chicken with baby mushrooms & sherry

Prepare the basic recipe, replacing the potatoes, olives, and orange zest with
1 1/4 cups sautéed whole baby mushrooms.

chicken thyme patties with potatoes, olives & sherry

Prepare the basic recipe, omitting the chicken thighs. Mix 3/4 cup ground
chicken, 1 egg, 3/4 cup bread crumbs, 1/2 teaspoon chopped fresh thyme,
and salt and pepper. Form into small patties. Fry in the same way as the
chicken thighs for about 3-4 minutes per side and continue cooking as in
the basic recipe.

chicken with potatoes, olives & port

Prepare the basic recipe, replacing the dry sherry and brandy with 1/2 cup
port for a richer dish.

chicken wings with honey & paprika

see base recipe page 112

chicken wings with herbs
Prepare the basic recipe, replacing the paprika with 1/2 teaspoon chopped fresh thyme and 1/2 teaspoon chopped fresh rosemary.

chicken wings with bloody mary marinade
Prepare the basic recipe, adding 1 tablespoon tomato paste, 1 tablespoon Worcestershire sauce, and 1 tablespoon red wine vinegar to the marinade.

fiery hot chicken wings
Prepare the basic recipe, adding 1/2 chopped fresh red chile and 1 teaspoon cayenne pepper to the marinade to get a very spicy version of this recipe.

smoky spicy chicken wings
Prepare the basic recipe, adding 1 tablespoon chipotle chile in adobo sauce for a more Mexican-style wing.

variations

duck breast with quince sauce

see base recipe page 115

duck breast with seasonal fruit sauce
Prepare the basic recipe, replacing the quince (which is a seasonal fruit) with either pears or apples. You need fruit that will keep its shape, so don't use any that becomes mushy when cooked.

chicken with quince sauce
Prepare the basic recipe, replacing the duck breast with chicken breast. Or you can use guinea fowl, if preferred.

duck breast with black cherry sauce
Prepare the basic recipe, replacing the quince with 3/4 cup pitted fresh black cherries. They are particularly good with duck.

duck breast with sauce à l'orange
Prepare the basic recipe, replacing the quince with thinly sliced segments from 1 orange, and adding 2 tablespoons Grand Marnier or Cointreau to the wine.

duck, beet & pickled walnut salad

see base recipe page 116

duck, beet, goat cheese & pickled walnut salad
Prepare the basic recipe, adding 3/4 cup crumbled goat cheese to the salad.
Choose a firm variety like a Bouchon de Chèvre, which is shaped like a log. Cut
off the skin before crumbling.

duck, beet, blue cheese & pickled walnut salad
Prepare the basic recipe, adding 3/4 cup crumbled blue cheese like Stilton.

duck, beet, & pickled walnut mesclun salad
Prepare the basic recipe, replacing the watercress and chicory with 2 heads
Little Gem lettuce (a miniature romaine) and a mesclun mix.

guinea fowl, beet & pickled walnut salad
Prepare the basic recipe, replacing the duck with guinea fowl breast, but make
sure you cook it for a little longer.

tapas de puerco
pork tapas

Pork puts on many guises through tapas, appearing as saucy meat balls and crackled belly pork, as tender loin and powerful chorizo, and most excitingly as morcilla sausage, served fried, with crisped edges and a smooth iron-rich center.

chorizo in red wine

see variations page 142

Baking slices of chorizo in red wine tenderizes the chorizo and also gives them a lovely winey kick. The heady rich sauce is just gorgeous sopped up with a chunk of crusty bread.

1/2 lb. semidry chorizo sausage, cut into
   3/4–inch-thick slices
1/3 cup dry red wine
2 fresh bay leaves

1 clove garlic, crushed
1 tbsp. good olive oil
sea salt and freshly ground black pepper

Preheat the oven to 400°F. Place all the ingredients in a shallow ovenproof dish. Bake for 15 minutes, until most of the wine has evaporated and the chorizo has begun to release its oil.

Serve hot in the dish with crusty bread to soak up the sauce.

Serves 4

morcilla with spicy peppers & quail eggs

see variations page 143

Morcilla (Spanish blood sausage) is one of the best blood sausages on the market. The best variety is the rice-filled one. Pairing it with spicy peppers and quail eggs is a very classic combination.

1/2 cup good olive oil	sea salt and freshly ground black pepper
6 whole piquillo peppers (from a jar)	14 oz. morcilla sausage, sliced into 4 rounds
1 clove garlic, crushed	4 fresh quail eggs

Over high heat, heat half the olive oil in a skillet, then add the peppers and garlic. Fry the peppers for 5–6 minutes until their skins begin to blister, stirring constantly to coat them all over in the oil and cook through. Remove from the heat, place on a serving plate, and sprinkle liberally with salt and pepper.

Add the rest of the oil to the pan and fry the sausage for 1 minute on each side. Add the eggs and fry for 1 minute, spooning hot oil over the yolks so they are cooked but still runny.

Serve the morcilla over the peppers with a quail egg on top.

Serves 4

pork meatballs in tomato sauce

see variations page 144

Every tapas restaurant tends to have a variation on this terrific meatballs dish. This recipe makes a small portion for tapas, but if you double the recipe and make smaller meatballs, you'll make a super sauce for pasta.

for the meatballs
9 oz. lean ground pork
1 small onion, finely chopped
2 cloves garlic, crushed and finely chopped
1/2 red chile, finely chopped
2 sprigs fresh rosemary, finely chopped
2 sprigs fresh thyme, finely chopped
1 1/2 cups fresh white bread crumbs
1 egg
3 tbsp. olive oil

for the tomato sauce
2 tbsp. olive oil
1 small onion, finely chopped
2 cloves garlic, chopped
7 tbsp. red wine
1 1/3 lbs. cherry tomatoes, chopped
1 bay leaf, crushed
1/2 tsp. sea salt
1/2 tsp. freshly ground black pepper

To make the meatballs, mix all the ingredients, except the oil, together in a large bowl, using your hands to combine evenly. Roll the mixture into 4 balls, about 1 1/2 inches in diameter, taking extra care to pack them tightly so they won't break apart during cooking. Set on a plate and place in the refrigerator to chill for 1/2 hour.

To make the sauce, heat half the oil in a heavy-bottomed, lidded saucepan, add the onion and garlic, and cook gently until transparent. Add the red wine and let simmer until reduced by half. Add the tomatoes, bay leaf, salt, and pepper. Bring the mixture to a boil and stir vigorously, breaking down the cherry tomatoes with the back of the spoon. Replace the lid and reduce the heat to a moderate simmer.

Once the meatballs have chilled, heat the remaining oil in a skillet. Brown the meatballs on all sides, then carefully add them to the tomato sauce. Turn the heat to a gentle boil and cook, uncovered, for 20 minutes, gently stirring halfway through. Serve immediately.

Serves 4

pork with morcilla & apples

see variations page 145

The combination of pork, morcilla, and apples is a pork lover's dream and a well-loved tapas dish, too. Iberico pork comes from the Spanish breed of black Iberian pig, whose unusual flavor is a result of the acorns in its diet. Good-quality pork loin will act as a more than adequate substitute, if pork fillet is unavailable.

3/4 lb. pork fillet (use Iberico if you can find it)
sea salt and freshly ground black pepper
4 tbsp. olive oil
3 fresh sage leaves

2 small Granny Smith apples, peeled, cored, and quartered
7 oz. morcilla (Spanish blood sausage), cut into 4 rounds
1/2 cup medium-dry white wine

Preheat the oven to 400°F. Pat dry and generously season the pork. Heat the oil in a heavy skillet and fry the sage leaves for 1 minute. Remove the sage from the pan and reserve. Cook the pork on all sides in the skillet until it has a deep golden color. Transfer the pork to a roasting pan and put in the oven for 10 minutes. Set the skillet aside while the pork is roasting.

Once the pork is cooked, remove from the oven and let rest for 10 minutes, covered with foil to keep the heat in. Carve the meat into slices and arrange on a serving plate. Meanwhile, return the skillet to medium heat and pan-fry the apples and morcilla, so that the apples caramelize and the sausage is cooked. Put them on the plate with the sliced pork and sage leaves. Deglaze the skillet with the wine, scraping up all the meaty particles into the sauce. Once the reduction is syrupy, pour it over the meats and apples, and serve immediately.

Serves 4

pork ribs in adobo barbecue sauce

see variations page 146

Slow-cooked pork ribs smothered in barbecue sauce and so well cooked they virtually fall off the bones. Need I say more?

1 tbsp. chipotle chile in adobo sauce
1 head garlic, cloves peeled
2 tsp. sweet smoked paprika
3 tbsp. tomato ketchup
1 tsp. ground cumin

2 tbsp. fresh oregano
2/3 cup cider vinegar
2/3 cup extra-virgin olive oil
sea salt and freshly ground black pepper
1 lb. pork ribs, cut into individual ribs

In a food processor, puree all the ingredients except the ribs until you get a completely smooth marinade.

Place the ribs in an airtight storage container and pour in the marinade, making sure all the ribs get a good coating. Place in the refrigerator to marinate for at least 2 hours but preferably overnight.

Preheat the oven to 300°F. Place the ribs and all the sauce in a deep roasting pan and cover with foil. Cook for 2 hours, until the meat is tender. Remove the foil and roast for another 1/2 hour until the sauce starts to caramelize and become sticky. Serve immediately with extra napkins for those sticky fingers.

Serves 4

roast pork with fennel & beans

see variations page 147

Slow-roasted pork belly with crisp crackling skin and meat that melts in your mouth has to be one of life's little food gifts, but paired with fennel it is simply divine.

1 (2 1/4–lb.) piece pork belly, rind scored
3 tsp. sea salt
1 onion, cut into eighths
1 leek, sliced into thick rounds
4 cloves garlic, peeled
1 sprig fresh sage
1 sprig fresh thyme
1 tbsp. fennel seeds, crushed

1/2 tsp. freshly ground black pepper
1 1/4 cups apple cider
2 1/2 cups homemade chicken stock
scant 1 cup water
2 (14–oz.) cans cannellini beans, rinsed and
    drained
1 tbsp. Dijon mustard
finely grated zest of 1 lemon

The night before, rub the pork belly all over with 2 teaspoons of the salt. Let sit in the refrigerator overnight. Preheat the oven to 450°F. Place the onion, leek, garlic, and herbs in the bottom of a roasting pan. Rub the pork with a cloth to remove most of the salt. Sprinkle with the remaining salt, crushed fennel seeds, and pepper. With your hands, really work the mixture into the skin and the meat. Place the pork on the bed of vegetables in the roasting pan, and bake for 30 minutes until the skin has crackled.

Reduce the oven temperature to 350°F. Pour the cider, stock, and water into the pan and bake for another 2 hours. Add more water as needed so the bottom doesn't burn. For the last 30 minutes, add the cannellini beans to the pan and stir well to coat in all the juices. Remove the pan from the oven, let the meat rest for 15 minutes before carving. Just before serving, stir the mustard and lemon zest through the hot beans.

Serves 4

cataplana

see variations page 148

Cataplana is a traditional Portuguese pork stew with garlic, wine, and clams, which is cooked in a special type of dish. Don't fear, though. I think it works perfectly well in a good Dutch oven or cast-iron pan with a lid.

5 cloves garlic, chopped
1 tbsp. sweet paprika
1/2 tsp. chili powder
sea salt
2/3 cup olive oil
5 1/2 oz. pork fillet, cut into 1/2-inch cubes

1 onion, finely chopped
scant 1 cup dry white wine
1/2 lb. quahog clams in the shell, scrubbed
2 tbsp. chopped fresh parsley
squeeze of lemon juice

Place the garlic, paprika, chili powder, salt, and half the olive oil in a food processor, and process to a paste. Marinate the pork in this mixture for at least 4 hours, or preferably overnight, stirring occasionally so all the meat gets a good coating.

Heat 3 tablespoons of the remaining olive oil in a wide saucepan with a well-fitting lid. Add the pork and all its marinade and cook over high heat for 5 minutes, stirring from time to time. Transfer the meat and sauce to a bowl and set aside. Add the rest of the oil to the pan, and fry the onion over medium-high heat for 5 minutes. Add the wine and bring to a boil for 1 minute. Return the pork to the pan, along with all the juices, stir well, then add the clams and replace the lid. Cook for 3–5 minutes, until the clams open. Discard any clams that do not open, stir through the parsley and a squeeze of lemon juice, and serve immediately.

Serves 4

chorizo, morcilla & fennel sausages with sticky balsamic onions

see variations page 149

Three different types of flavorful Mediterranean sausage served with sticky balsamic onions. Bliss.

2 tbsp. balsamic vinegar
2 tbsp. extra-virgin olive oil
2 cloves garlic, completely crushed
1 tsp. dark brown sugar
2 sprigs fresh marjoram, chopped
sea salt and freshly ground black pepper

1 red onion, cut into 8 pieces
1 raw chorizo sausage, chopped in 4 pieces
4 baby morcilla sausages
1 fennel sausage, chopped in 4 pieces

Preheat the oven to 375°F. In a large bowl, mix the balsamic vinegar, half the oil, the garlic, brown sugar, marjoram, salt, and pepper. Mix thoroughly, then add the onions and mix again, making sure the onions are evenly coated.

Pour the mixture into a roasting pan. At the same time, place the sausages in a separate pan and drizzle with the remaining olive oil. Bake both pans in the oven for 25 minutes, turning the onions over halfway through, and giving the sausage pan a good shake. If the balsamic marinade begins to burn, add 2–3 tablespoons of water to the pan.

Spoon the hot onions into individual dishes with one of each of the types of sausage and top with a spoonful of the balsamic marinade.

Serves 4

variations

chorizo in red wine

see base recipe page 127

chorizo & chile in red wine
Prepare the basic recipe, adding 1 sliced red chile with the garlic.

chorizo & chile in white wine
Prepare the basic recipe, replacing the red wine with white wine for a lighter dish.

chorizo & chile in white wine & saffron
Prepare the basic recipe, replacing the red wine with white wine and adding a small pinch of saffron with the garlic.

morcilla in red wine
Prepare the basic recipe, replacing the chorizo with morcilla (Spanish blood sausage).

morcilla with spicy peppers & quail eggs

see base recipe page 129

morcilla with pimientos de padrón & quail eggs
Prepare the basic recipe, replacing the piquillo peppers with 2–3 pimientos de Padrón.

morcilla with chanterelle mushrooms & duck eggs
Prepare the basic recipe, replacing the peppers with 2–3 sliced chanterelle mushrooms and the quail eggs with duck eggs.

morcilla with crisp sage, duck eggs & truffle oil
Prepare the basic recipe, replacing the peppers with 6 sage leaves. Gently fry the sage in the oil, removing it to drain on paper towels as it begins to crisp. Replace the quail eggs with duck eggs, and drizzle 1 teaspoon truffle oil over the assembled dish.

chorizo with spicy peppers & quail eggs
Prepare the basic recipe, replacing the morcilla with chorizo.

variations

pork meatballs in tomato sauce

see base recipe page 130

pork meatballs in tomato sauce with olives
Prepare the basic recipe, adding 1 rounded tablespoon pitted black olives
to the tomato sauce.

pork meatballs in tomato sauce with capers
Prepare the basic recipe, adding 1 rounded tablespoon capers to the
tomato sauce.

beef meatballs in spicy tomato sauce
Prepare the basic recipe, replacing the pork with ground beef and adding
1 chopped red chile with the onion to the tomato sauce.

turkey meatballs in tomato sauce with basil
Prepare the basic recipe, replacing the pork with ground turkey and adding a
few fresh basil leaves to the tomato sauce for the last minute of cooking.

pork with morcilla & apples

see base recipe page 133

pork with chorizo & apples
Prepare the basic recipe, replacing the morcilla with raw chorizo.

pork with morcilla & pears
Prepare the basic recipe, replacing the apples with pears.

pork with chorizo & pears
Prepare the basic recipe, replacing the morcilla and apples with raw chorizo
and pears.

pork with morcilla, white beans & apples
Prepare the basic recipe, adding 1 (7-ounce) can white beans to the skillet
along with the apples and morcilla.

variations

pork ribs in adobo barbecue sauce

see base recipe page 134

pork ribs in pineapple-adobo barbecue sauce
Prepare the basic recipe, adding 7 tablespoons pineapple juice to the sauce.

pork ribs in mango-adobo barbecue sauce
Prepare the basic recipe, adding 7 tablespoons mango juice and 1 tablespoon mango chutney to the sauce.

pork ribs in extra-spicy adobo barbecue sauce
Prepare the basic recipe, adding 1/3 cup hot chili sauce to the sauce.

spice-rubbed pork ribs in adobo barbecue sauce
Prepare the basic recipe, but rub the pork ribs with 1 teaspoon ground coriander and 1 teaspoon ground cumin before coating with the sauce.

variations

roast pork with fennel & beans

see base recipe page 137

roast pork with fennel, pancetta & beans
Prepare the basic recipe, adding 4 tablespoons fried cubed pancetta with the onion.

roast pork with fennel, chorizo & beans
Prepare the basic recipe, adding 4 tablespoons fried chopped chorizo with the onion.

roast pork with caraway & lentils
Prepare the basic recipe, replacing the fennel seeds with caraway seeds, and the cannellini beans with lentils.

roast pork with five-spice & butternut squash puree
Prepare the basic recipe, replacing the fennel seeds with 1 tablespoon five-spice powder. Peel 1/2 pound butternut squash and roast with 1 tablespoon olive oil in a separate roasting pan for the last 40 minutes that the pork is cooking. Puree the squash with 1/4 cup milk and serve with the pork.

variations

cataplana

see base recipe page 138

pork stew with chorizo, garlic, wine & clams
Prepare the basic recipe, adding 1 chopped, small semidry chorizo when cooking the onion.

pork stew with chile, garlic, wine & clams
Prepare the basic recipe, adding 1 chopped, small red chile when cooking the onion.

pork stew with saffron, garlic, wine & clams
Prepare the basic recipe, adding a small pinch of saffron when cooking the onion.

pork stew with chorizo, saffron, garlic, wine & mussels
Prepare the basic recipe, replacing the clams with mussels, and adding 1 chopped, small semidry chorizo and a small pinch of saffron when cooking the onion.

variations

chorizo, morcilla & fennel sausages with sticky balsamic onions

see base recipe page 141

chorizo with sticky balsamic onions
Prepare the basic recipe, replacing the morcilla and fennel sausages with 2 extra chorizo sausages.

morcilla with sticky balsamic onions
Prepare the basic recipe, replacing the chorizo and fennel sausages with 8 extra morcilla sausages.

fennel sausages with sticky balsamic onions
Prepare the basic recipe, replacing the morcilla and chorizo sausages with 2 extra fennel sausages.

chorizo, morcilla & fennel sausages with sticky wine onions
Prepare the basic recipe, adding 2 tablespoons red wine to the balsamic marinade.

tapas de cordero
lamb tapas

Earthy lamb in tender cutlets or slow roasted shoulders, delicate fillets or hearty kebabs, with subtle spicing or powerful herbs, always makes for delicious and satisfying tapas.

grilled lamb cutlets with burnt butter, rosemary & capers

see variations page 167

Lamb cutlets are a ready-made finger food, with their own holders making them a really fun addition to your tapas menu. This recipe shows off lamb at its best. Get a rack of lamb that's either middle neck, which is cheaper with more flavor but only five bones, or the best end of neck, which is more delicate and more expensive, with eight bones.

1 rack of lamb
sea salt and freshly ground black pepper
1/2 tbsp. olive oil
4 tbsp. (1/2 stick) sweet butter

1 small sprig fresh rosemary
1 heaping tbsp. capers (I prefer capers in vinegar to salted)
juice of 1/2 lemon

Carve the lamb into individual cutlets. If the cutlets are really thick, you can pound them with a meat mallet to thin them out a bit, but I like them about 1/2 inch thick. Season with salt and pepper and rub with the oil. Heat a griddle pan on high heat until smoking. Cook the cutlets for 2–3 minutes on each side, remove from pan, and let rest.

In a small saucepan, melt the butter and add the rosemary. When it starts to foam, it will start to turn a nutty color. Add the capers, fry for 30 seconds, and then pour in the lemon juice. Remove pan from the heat and season with salt and pepper. Place the lamb in a serving dish and pour in the juices and burnt butter sauce.

Serves 4

mallorcan slow-roasted lamb shoulder

see variations page 168

This classic dish is normally made using milk-fed baby lambs. Most butchered lambs are around a year of age and on a solid diet, making their meat darker and richer. Milk-fed lamb is therefore hard to find. This recipe calls for half a lamb shoulder, making it the perfect size to bring to the table and tear apart.

1/2 shoulder of lamb, weighing about 2 lbs., on the bone
2 carrots
2 celery stalks
1 leek
2 onions
1 (14-oz.) can plum tomatoes with juice

3 whole garlic heads, halved, and papery skin removed
1 cup white wine
a few sprigs fresh thyme, rosemary, and parsley tied together
1 1/4 cups chicken stock

Heat the oven to 325°F. On top of the stove, carefully brown the shoulder all over in a roasting pan to get some color on the lamb and to render the fat a little. Remove the lamb and discard all but a couple of tablespoons of the fat. Chop the carrots, celery, leek, and onions into 1 1/2-inch chunks. Add them to the pan and brown all over. Add the tomatoes, garlic, wine, herbs, and stock, then put the lamb back in the pan.

Loosely cover the pan with a sheet of buttered parchment paper and cook in the oven for about 3 hours (check after 2 1/2). When it's falling off the bone, it's ready to serve.

Serves 4

lamb fillet with tzatziki

see variations page 169

The buttery texture of lamb fillet that's been spiked with red chile, spices, and garlic and complemented with the Greek yogurt-based appetizer "tzatziki" makes for a scrumptious tapas.

1/2 tbsp. olive oil
2 cardamom pods, crushed
1 tsp. ground cumin
1 clove garlic, crushed
1 red chile, finely chopped
1/2 small bunch fresh mint
1 lamb fillet, about 10 1/2 oz., trimmed of fat

for the tzatziki
1/2 cucumber, cut into small dice
2/3 cup fat-free Greek yogurt
sea salt and freshly ground black pepper
1/2 bunch fresh mint, finely chopped
extra-virgin olive oil for drizzling

Pound the oil, cardamom, cumin, garlic, chile, and mint in a mortar and pestle. Rub mixture all over the lamb. Let this marinate for about 2 hours.

Mix the cucumber into the yogurt and season with plenty of salt and pepper and the mint.

Meanwhile, heat a griddle pan on high heat until almost smoking. Wipe off any excess marinade and cook the lamb in a dry pan on all sides until it is browned and feels firm to the touch. Let rest for a couple of minutes, then slice. Spread a layer of the cucumber yogurt on a serving plate and top with the lamb and a drizzle of olive oil.

Serves 4

lamb ragout with polenta

see variations page 170

A really fragrant southern Spanish lamb stew that's shredded and served with polenta.

1 tbsp. olive oil
14 oz. lamb shoulder meat, cubed
1 onion, chopped
1 carrot, peeled and chopped
1 celery stalk, chopped
4 cloves garlic, chopped
1 tbsp. tomato paste
1 bay leaf
really good pinch saffron
good pinch smoked paprika
few fresh thyme sprigs, chopped

fresh rosemary sprig, finely chopped
few fresh parsley sprigs, chopped
1 3/4 cups white wine
1 3/4 cups lamb or chicken stock
1 (14–oz.) can chopped tomatoes
for the polenta
1 generous cup hot chicken stock
1/2 cup instant polenta
1/4 cup freshly grated Parmesan cheese
4 tbsp. (1/2 stick) unsalted butter

Preheat the oven to 325°F. Heat the olive oil in a heavy-duty Dutch oven, then cook the meat in batches until golden brown all over. Transfer the meat with a slotted spoon to a bowl. Add the onions, carrots, and celery to the pan and cook on a fairly low heat for 15 minutes or until the vegetables have softened and become slightly golden. For the last 2 minutes of cooking, add the garlic.

Stir in the tomato paste and cook for another minute. Add the bay leaf, saffron, paprika, thyme, rosemary, wine, stock, tomatoes, and half the parsley. Put the meat and all of its juices back into the pan. Give it a good stir, then put the lid on and place in the oven for 2 hours. The meat should be really soft and the sauce thick and rich.

Let the casserole rest outside the oven for 10 minutes, then go into it with two forks and shred the meat to bits. Meanwhile, make the polenta by bringing the stock to a rolling boil and pouring the polenta into it, stirring constantly. Continue cooking for 2 minutes, then remove the pan from the heat and beat in the cheese and butter. Season really well. You want it quite soft and smooth. Serve with the casserole in a large tapas bowl, topped with the remaining parsley.

Serves 4

roast lamb with pomegranate salad

see variations page 171

This healthier take on roast lamb makes a scrumptious and piquant tapas. The fattiness of lamb is smoothed with the acidic pomegranate in the salad, glaze, and gravy.

4 tbsp. pomegranate molasses
1 tsp. ground cumin
juice of 1 lemon
1 tbsp. olive oil
2 cloves garlic, minced
1 onion, roughly chopped
1/4 shoulder of lamb, weighing about 2 lbs., on the bone, lightly scored

1 1/4 cups chicken or lamb stock
for the salad
seeds of 1 pomegranate
handful fresh flat-leaf parsley
4 oz. watercress
1 small red onion, finely chopped
1 tbsp. extra-virgin olive oil

Heat oven to 325°F. In a small bowl, mix the molasses with the cumin, lemon juice, olive oil, and garlic. Scatter the onions over the bottom of a casserole dish or a deep roasting pan. Place the lamb on top of the onions. Pour the glaze over the lamb and rub it in a little. Rinse the bowl out with the stock, then pour it around — not over — the lamb.

Cover the dish with a lid or the pan with a large piece of foil. Roast the lamb, undisturbed, for 3 hours, then remove the lid or foil and continue to roast for 30 minutes more to give the lamb color. When the lamb has finished cooking, pour off the juices, remove as much fat as possible, and pour the juices back over the lamb. Just before serving, gently toss all the salad ingredients together. Serve the lamb with its sauce, accompanied by the salad.

Serves 4

lamb pilaf

see variations page 172

Classically a Middle Eastern dish, this fragrant rice dish is great for sharing. Spiced with cinnamon, coriander, and cloves, and studded with sweet apricots, this dish is scrumptious.

small handful pine nuts or slivered almonds
1 tbsp. olive oil
1 onion, halved and sliced
1/2 tsp. ground coriander
1 cinnamon stick, broken in half
2 whole cloves

10 oz. cubed stewing lamb
3/4 cup basmati rice
1 1/4 cups lamb or vegetable stock
6–8 dried apricots
sea salt and freshly ground black pepper
handful fresh mint leaves, roughly chopped

Dry-fry the pine nuts or almonds in a large pan until lightly toasted, then tip onto a plate. Add the oil to the pan, then fry the onion, ground coriander, cinnamon, and cloves together until they start to turn golden. Raise the heat, stir in the lamb, and fry until the meat changes color. Add the rice and cook for 1 minute, stirring all the time.

Add the stock, apricots, salt, and pepper. Turn the heat down, cover, and simmer for 12 minutes until the rice is tender and the stock has been absorbed. Toss in the nuts and mint and serve.

Serves 4

pan-fried lamb cutlets with herbed bread crumbs

see variations page 173

I first came across this dish as an appetizer in an Italian restaurant many years ago, but it makes the most wonderful tapas. Expect pink lamb, surrounded by crisp fragrant crumbs dotted with capers and herbs.

1 rack of lamb
3/4 cup flour
sea salt and freshly ground black pepper
1 large free-range egg, lightly beaten

2 cups fresh bread crumbs
small handful fresh mint, finely chopped
1 tbsp. capers, finely chopped
1/2 cup olive oil

Cut the lamb into cutlets, then place a double sheet of plastic wrap over each one and pound with a mallet to flatten a bit. Keep in mind you still want them to be about 1/4 inch thick, rather than really thin like a scallop. Place the flour (which you should season with lots of salt and pepper), the egg, and the bread crumbs in separate bowls. Add the chopped mint and capers to the bread crumbs and mix thoroughly.

Dip each cutlet into the flour, then the egg (coating them very well, as this will act like a glue), and finally into the bread crumbs. Set the breaded cutlets aside for a few minutes. Heat the oil in a skillet, then lay each breaded cutlet in the hot fat. Cook for 2 minutes on each side or until the crumb coating has turned golden brown. You want the cutlets to be pink inside, so be careful not to overcook them. Drain them on paper towels and place on a serving dish.

Serves 4

marinated lamb kebabs with zesty fava beans

see variations page 174

It cannot be denied that kebabs of tender chunks of marinated and lightly charred lamb are always a pleasing prospect. Yet when served on top of emerald green fava beans with a zingy lemony dressing, this dish takes on elegance far beyond the common kebab.

juice and zest of 1 lemon
1/2 cup olive oil
sea salt and freshly ground black pepper
1/4 cup finely chopped fresh mint leaves

1/4 cup finely chopped fresh parsley
10 oz. lamb fillet, cut into 3/4-inch cubes
1 cup shelled fava beans

In a deep bowl, whisk together half the lemon juice and zest, half the olive oil, and salt and pepper, until the mixture is emulsified. Add half the herbs and then toss the lamb through the mixture. Let marinate for at least 2 hours, but preferably overnight.

Bring a deep pan of salted water to a boil, add the fava beans, and cook for 3 minutes until the beans are soft. Drain, and when cool enough to handle, remove the tough outer skins. Place in a bowl and pour in the remaining olive oil, lemon juice and zest, and herbs. Season with salt and pepper.

Thread 3 or 4 chunks of meat onto each of 4 skewers. On a very hot grill or griddle pan, cook the meat, turning every 30 seconds, until done. Place each kebab on a small serving of zesty fava beans and serve immediately.

Serves 4

spiced lamb meatballs with crushed pistachios

see variations page 175

Meaty little balls with a fragrant selection of whole spices and the unexpected crunch of bright green pistachio nuts. Delicious!

1 small clove garlic, roughly chopped
1/2 small onion, roughly chopped
2 tbsp. shelled pistachios
1 tsp. cumin seeds
1/2 tsp. coriander seeds

1/2 tsp. fennel seeds
1/4 tsp. dried red pepper flakes
sea salt and freshly ground black pepper
1/2 lb. ground lamb
2 tbsp. olive oil

In a food processor, pulse all the ingredients except the lamb and oil, until you get a coarse mixture. In a deep bowl, add the lamb to the mixture using your hands, mixing until it is well combined. Roll about a tablespoon of the mixture in your hands until it comes together in a tight ball, about 1 1/4 inches in diameter.

Add the oil to a nonstick skillet over medium-high heat, and carefully fry the meatballs for 5 minutes, making sure you cook them on all sides. Serve immediately.

Serves 4

grilled lamb cutlets with burnt butter, rosemary & capers

see base recipe page 151

grilled lamb cutlets with burnt butter, rosemary, anchovies & capers
Prepare the basic recipe, adding 4 canned anchovies to the butter while you are burning it.

grilled lamb cutlets with burnt butter, fennel & capers
Prepare the basic recipe, omitting the rosemary and adding 1 teaspoon crushed fennel seeds to the foaming butter.

grilled lamb cutlets with burnt butter, rosemary, garlic & capers
Prepare the basic recipe, adding 1–2 crushed cloves of garlic to the pan with the butter.

grilled lamb cutlets with burnt butter, mint & capers
Prepare the basic recipe, replacing the rosemary with a few sprigs of fresh mint.

mallorcan slow-roasted lamb shoulder

see base recipe page 153

mallorcan slow-roasted lamb shoulder with white beans
Prepare the basic recipe, adding 2 (14-ounce) cans of cannellini beans, rinsed and drained, for the last 30 minutes of cooking.

mallorcan slow-roasted lamb shoulder with red wine
Prepare the basic recipe, replacing the white wine with red wine.

mallorcan slow-roasted lamb shoulder with orzo
Prepare the basic recipe, adding 10 ounces Greek orzo for the last 30 minutes of cooking.

mallorcan slow-roasted lamb shoulder with gravy
Prepare the basic recipe, but when the lamb is cooked, remove it from the pan and set it aside, covered. Strain out the vegetables and push them through a fine sieve, stirring the resulting puree back into the pan with the saved juices. Turn the heat up to medium high and reduce to a thick gravy. Serve with the lamb.

lamb fillet with tzatziki

see base recipe page 154

lamb fillet with spicy tzatziki
Prepare the basic recipe, adding 2 seeded green chiles, grilled until the skin is blackened. Chop finely and add to the cucumber yogurt sauce.

lemony lamb fillet with tzatziki
Prepare the basic recipe, adding the juice and zest of 1 lemon to the marinade and 1 teaspoon lemon zest to the yogurt sauce.

lamb & cucumber yogurt pita sandwiches
Prepare the basic recipe, but chop the marinated lamb into chunks and thread onto kebab skewers. Cook for 30 seconds per side. Add 2 chopped scallions to the yogurt sauce. Spread the sauce inside 4 mini pita breads and add the lamb chunks.

lamb fillet with herbs & cucumber-lime yogurt
Prepare the basic recipe, adding the zest and juice of 1 lime to the yogurt sauce.

lamb ragout with polenta

see base recipe page 156

lamb ragout with tomatoes & white wine with polenta
Prepare the basic recipe, omitting the saffron and smoked paprika.

lamb ragout with creamy mashed potatoes
Prepare the basic recipe, replacing the polenta with very rich mashed potatoes made with butter and whipping cream.

lamb ragout with herbed polenta
Prepare the basic recipe, adding 2 tablespoons chopped fresh herbs like basil, parsley, and mint to the polenta before serving.

lamb ragout with red wine & polenta
Prepare the basic recipe, omitting the saffron, paprika, and tomatoes and replacing the white wine with 1 3/4 cups red wine. Add 3 whole cloves when the wine is added.

variations

roast lamb with pomegranate salad

see base recipe page 158

roast lamb with pomegranate & orange salad
Prepare the basic recipe, adding the segments of 1 orange to the salad.

five-spice roast lamb with pomegranate salad
Prepare the basic recipe, replacing the cumin with 1 teaspoon
five-spice powder.

fragrant roast lamb with pomegranate salad
Prepare the basic recipe, adding 1/2 teaspoon crushed toasted coriander seeds
and a pinch of dried red pepper flakes to the glaze.

roast duck with pomegranate salad
Prepare the basic recipe, replacing the lamb shoulder with 2 duck legs.

lamb pilaf

see base recipe page 161

chicken pilaf
Prepare the basic recipe, replacing the lamb with the same weight of boneless chicken thighs and the stock with chicken stock.

lamb pilaf with prunes
Prepare the basic recipe, replacing the apricots with prunes.

lamb pilaf with lemon
Prepare the basic recipe, omitting the apricots and adding 1 sliced lemon.

indian lamb pilaf
Prepare the basic recipe, adding 1 teaspoon ground cumin and 1/2 teaspoon ground turmeric with the rest of the spices. Omit the apricots.

variations

pan-fried lamb cutlets with herbed bread crumbs

see base recipe page 162

pan-fried lamb cutlets with bread crumbs
Prepare the basic recipe, omitting the mint and capers.

pan-fried lamb cutlets with mustard & herb bread crumbs
Prepare the basic recipe, spreading each lamb cutlet with 1/4 teaspoon Dijon mustard before coating with flour.

pan-fried lamb cutlets with spicy bread crumbs
Prepare the basic recipe, omitting the mint and capers and adding 1 tablespoon chopped fresh cilantro and 1/2 teaspoon curry powder to the bread crumbs.

pan-fried lamb cutlets with salsa verde bread crumbs
Prepare the basic recipe, adding 1 tablespoon mixed fresh herbs like tarragon, parsley, and basil and 2 chopped cornichons to the bread crumbs.

variations

marinated lamb kebabs with zesty fava beans

see base recipe page 165

spicy marinated lamb kebabs with zesty fava beans & fennel
Prepare the basic recipe, replacing the herbs in the marinade with
1/2 teaspoon dried red pepper flakes. Toss 1/2 cup very finely sliced fennel
with the dressed fava beans.

rose harissa marinated lamb kebabs with fava beans
Prepare the basic recipe, replacing the herbs in the marinade with 1 heaping
teaspoon of rose harissa.

garlic & rosemary marinated lamb kebabs with fava beans & anchovies
Prepare the basic recipe, replacing the herbs in the marinade with 1 very
finely crushed clove garlic and 1/2 teaspoon fresh rosemary. Mash 2 canned
anchovies with the back of a fork and mix into the dressed fava beans.

cumin lamb kebabs on griddled zucchini
Prepare the basic recipe, omitting the herbs and the fava beans. Add
1/2 teaspoon ground cumin to the marinade. Thinly slice 1 small zucchini,
brush with 1 tablespoon olive oil, and griddle for 1 minute per side. Remove
from the pan and drizzle with a second tablespoon of olive oil. Serve the
lamb kebabs on top of the zucchini.

spiced lamb meatballs with crushed pistachios

see base recipe page 166

herbed lamb meatballs with crushed pistachios
Prepare the basic recipe, omitting the cumin, coriander, fennel, and red pepper flakes, and adding 2 tablespoons of roughly chopped fresh mint and 1 tablespoon chopped fresh thyme.

lamb meatballs with lemon & anchovies
Prepare the basic recipe, omitting the pistachios, cumin, coriander, fennel, and red pepper flakes, and adding the zest of 1 lemon and 2 canned anchovy fillets.

spiced lamb meatballs with apricots
Prepare the basic recipe, replacing the pistachios with 1 tablespoon finely chopped dried apricots.

lamb meatballs with pine nuts & feta
Prepare the basic recipe, omitting the pistachios, cumin, coriander, and red pepper flakes, and adding 4 tablespoons pine nuts to the food processor and 4 tablespoons crumbled feta to the bowl with the lamb.

lamb meatballs with kalamata olives
Prepare the basic recipe, omitting the pistachios, cumin, coriander, and fennel, and adding 3 tablespoons pitted kalamata olives and the zest of 1/2 lemon.

tapas de carne
beef tapas

Beef, from blue to lingeringly slow cooked over hours, it never fails to excite the taste buds. This versatile meat really comes in to its own with tapas being both alluring and so easy to cook well.

beef carpaccio with anchovy mayo & crispy garlic

see variations page 193

This Italian classic has had a Spanish makeover with anchovy mayo and crisped garlic.

1/3 lb. beef fillet, trimmed
2 free-range egg yolks
1 heaping tsp. Dijon mustard
1 tsp. white wine vinegar
sea salt and freshly ground black pepper
8 anchovy fillets in oil, mashed to a paste

1 1/4 cups vegetable oil
juice of 1 lemon
3 tbsp. olive oil
5 large cloves garlic, sliced
good handful watercress or arugula leaves,
    dressed in lemon juice and olive oil

Wrap beef tightly in plastic wrap and place in freezer for 1/2 hour. To make the mayonnaise, put the egg yolks in a deep bowl and add the mustard, vinegar, salt, pepper, and anchovies. Mix well. With a whisk, mix in the vegetable oil, a drop at a time. Once you've added about a quarter of the oil, the mixture will begin to thicken. Add the rest of the vegetable oil in a thin stream, whisking all the time, until you have a thick smooth mayonnaise. Finish by squeezing in the lemon juice. Chill until you are ready to serve.

To make the crispy garlic, heat the olive oil in a heavy pan over high heat until the surface of the oil shimmers. Add the garlic and let sizzle for about 30 seconds, until just crisp and light golden brown. Remove from the oil and drain on paper towels. Remove the beef from the freezer and, with a very sharp knife, slice as thin as you can. Lay slices neatly on plates and top with mayonnaise, crisp garlic, and the dressed watercress or arugula.

Serves 4

beef tenderloin with rioja & blue cheese

see variations page 194

A rich red wine reduction dresses and glosses beef tenderloin while the blue cheese slowly oozes as it melts against the meat. Rioja is a quintessentially Spanish wine and a perfect partner for beef tenderloin.

2 1/4 cups Rioja red wine
2/3 cup olive oil
2 cloves garlic, chopped
sea salt and freshly ground black pepper
1 1/4 lbs. beef tenderloin

2 tbsp. light brown sugar
1 cinnamon stick
1/2 tsp. dried red pepper flakes
5 1/2 oz. blue cheese, such as Stilton,
    crumbled, for serving

In a deep bowl, whisk 3 tablespoons red wine with 2 tablespoons oil, garlic, and salt and pepper until the mixture is emulsified. Cut beef into 16 equal-sized pieces, add to the marinade, and stir in. Cover and leave in the refrigerator overnight.

In a heavy pan, make the sauce. Boil together the remaining wine, sugar, cinnamon stick, and red pepper flakes. Place over a moderate heat and simmer briskly, stirring until the wine is reduced to a thin syrup. Heat a griddle pan until very hot and almost smoking. Toss the meat to coat in the remaining oil, and cook until the outside is scored with deep chars and the inside is pink (medium-rare). Tumble the meat through the Rioja reduction and pile onto a serving plate with a good crumbling of the blue cheese.

Serves 4

beef skewers with béarnaise sauce

see variations page 195

It's still the simplest of tapas that are the crowd-pleasers, and grilled beef skewers dipped into a classic béarnaise sauce could please a stadium.

1 shallot, finely chopped
2 sprigs fresh tarragon
4 tbsp. dry white wine
2 tbsp. white wine vinegar
3 1/2 tbsp. water
3/4 cup (1 1/2 sticks) unsalted butter

3 free-range egg yolks
1/2 lb. sirloin steak, cut into 3/4-inch cubes
4 wooden skewers, soaked in water for 1 hour
1 tbsp. olive oil
sea salt and freshly ground black pepper

To make the béarnaise, mix the shallot, tarragon, wine, white wine vinegar, and water in a saucepan. Boil until reduced by two-thirds. Pour through a sieve, reserving all the juice and discarding the tarragon and shallot. Allow to cool slightly. Then, melt the butter in a pan over a low heat, until liquid. Turn up the heat and let butter boil for 30 seconds, then pour the clear liquid into a measuring cup and discard the milky residue at the bottom of the pan. With a hand whisk, whisk the egg yolks and wine reduction together. Slowly, still whisking, add the butter in a thin, steady stream, until a medium-thick sauce has formed. Cover and set aside until the steak is cooked.

Meanwhile, heat a griddle pan or a barbecue grill until really hot and almost smoking. Thread the steak pieces equally among the wooden skewers. Drizzle with the olive oil, and sprinkle with salt and pepper. Lay the skewers on the griddle or grill and cook for 1 minute on each of the 4 sides. Serve the skewers piled up together on one big platter with a bowl of the béarnaise to dip into.

Serves 4

ribeye with peppers & polenta fries

see variations page 196

Sometimes it's nice to look at tapas as simply a plate to share, so turning up at the table with a large carved beef rib and fries is a treat for guests. Polenta fries are the new craze on the block and the Spanish twist is added with melt-in-the-mouth piquillo peppers.

for the polenta fries
1 tbsp. olive oil
2 1/2 cups chicken or vegetable stock
3/5 cup (5 1/2 oz.) instant polenta
4 tbsp. finely grated Parmesan cheese
2 tbsp. (1/4 stick) butter
sea salt and freshly ground black pepper
3 tbsp. vegetable oil

3 tbsp. flour
for the steak and peppers
1/2 lb. ribeye steak, at room temperature
sea salt and freshly ground black pepper
2 tbsp. olive oil
1 clove garlic, crushed
4 oz. canned piquillo peppers, drained

For the polenta, grease a 9 x 12–inch baking pan with the olive oil. Bring the stock to a boil in a large saucepan. Gradually add the polenta, whisking constantly until well mixed. Lower the heat and cook, stirring constantly. In 2 minutes the mixture should thicken and the polenta should be soft. Remove from the heat and stir in the Parmesan, butter, and salt and pepper. Pour the polenta evenly into the prepared baking pan and smooth the surface, patting gently with the back of a spoon. Cover and refrigerate for 4 hours or overnight.

Turn cold polenta onto a clean cutting board. Cut into strips, 3/4 inch wide by 3 inches long. Heat the vegetable oil in a large nonstick skillet. Toss the polenta strips in the flour until thoroughly coated. Add the polenta in batches to the oil and fry for 5 minutes or until golden brown on each side. Use a slotted spoon to transfer polenta fries to a plate lined with paper towels. Keep warm.

For the steak, set a griddle pan on high heat until the pan is very hot. Season beef with salt, rub with a little of the olive oil, and cook, turning after 2–3 minutes, until the outside is charred and the inside is medium-rare. Remove from heat and let rest while you cook the peppers. For the peppers, warm the remaining olive oil in a saucepan over low-medium heat, add garlic, and stir to infuse the flavor. Add peppers and stir until they bleed into the oil. Some will stay whole and some will mush up. Season with sea salt and pepper. Slice the meat thickly and serve on a board topped with the peppers and a pile of polenta fries.

Serves 4

flap steak with bone marrow

see variations page 197

Flap steak is a cut of steak taken from the side of the animal. It tends to be underused outside of France (where it's known as bavette d'aloyau), which is a shame because it's one of the most delicious beef cuts. Shallots and roasted bone marrow complement the meat, producing a modern tapas classic.

2 pieces veal or beef marrow bones, each 2–3
   inches long and split down the middle
sea salt and freshly ground pepper
2 tbsp. (1/4 stick) butter
8 small shallots, trimmed and peeled
1 tbsp. red wine vinegar

1 1/4 cups red wine
sea salt and freshly ground pepper
1 fresh bay leaf, bruised
1 3/4 cups homemade beef stock
1/2 lb. flap steak
1 tbsp. olive oil

Preheat the oven to 375°F. Place the marrow bones, marrow side up, in a roasting pan, and season with salt and pepper. Place in the oven for 20 minutes, until the marrow is loose and soft, without melting away. In a small saucepan, melt the butter, then brown the whole shallots until they are caramelized on all sides. Add the wine vinegar, red wine, salt, pepper, bay leaf, and stock, and simmer for 10 minutes. Once the sauce is syrupy, remove from the heat and discard the bay leaf. Keep warm.

Season the steak with salt and pepper, then rub with olive oil. Heat a griddle or barbecue grill until smoking, then cook the steak for 3 minutes per side for medium-rare. Allow the steak to rest, covered, for 10 minutes. Slice the steak across the grain, place on a serving plate with the roasted marrow, and pour the sauce and any of the marrow oil on top.

Serves 4

rich oxtail stew with parsnip puree

see variations page 198

The great thing about oxtail is that it makes a perfect tapas portion when serving only one or two bones. Served with a delicate parsnip puree, this will be one of the dishes that you might just want to serve as a full-sized portion.

for the oxtail stew
2 tbsp. olive oil
2 1/4 lbs. oxtails, cut into 2-inch lengths and trimmed of excess fat
8 shallots, peeled
2 large cloves garlic, crushed
1 tbsp. tomato paste
1 celery stalk, finely chopped
1 carrot, finely chopped
2 1/4 cups red wine

2 1/2 cups homemade beef stock
1 tbsp. finely chopped fresh thyme
1 bay leaf
1 tbsp. chopped fresh parsley
sea salt and freshly ground black pepper
for the parsnip puree
3 large parsnips, peeled and chopped
2 tbsp. (1/4 stick) butter
1/4 cup whipping cream
sea salt and freshly ground black pepper

Preheat the oven to 275°F. Heat the oil in a large Dutch oven. Over high heat, brown the oxtails on all sides, in batches if necessary. Transfer to a plate and set aside. Caramelize the shallots in the fat remaining in the pan, then add the garlic and tomato paste. Cook, stirring for a minute, then return the browned oxtails to the pan with the celery, carrot, wine, beef stock, thyme, bay leaf, parsley, salt, and pepper. Bring to a boil, cover, and place in the oven for 3 hours. The meat is cooked when it is falling off the bone and the sauce is thick and reduced. Cook the parsnips in boiling salted water until tender. Drain, then add to a blender with the butter, whipping cream, salt, and pepper, and blend until smooth. Serve on the bone or shred the meat off the bone. Serve the parsnip puree in a serving dish, topped with the stew.

Serves 4

veal milanese with sage & anchovies

see variations page 199

Veal, sage, and anchovies are a marriage made in heaven, so imagine this... Breaded veal escalope pan-fried and dressed with crispy sage and anchovy sandwiches and doused in lemon. Scrumptious!

4 small veal escalopes
1 large free-range egg
2 tbsp. flour, seasoned with salt and pepper
3 cups fresh white bread crumbs
4 tbsp. (1/2 stick) butter

4 tbsp. olive oil
12 canned anchovy fillets
24 small fresh sage leaves
1 lemon, quartered

Make the escalopes thinner by placing them between pieces of plastic wrap and gently beating them with a rolling pin or meat mallet. Beat the egg in a shallow bowl. Put the flour and bread crumbs into separate bowls. Dip each escalope, first into the flour, then the beaten egg, and then into the bread crumbs. Heat the butter and oil in a large skillet over medium-high heat. When really hot, add the escalopes to the skillet. Cook them for 3–4 minutes on each side or until crisp and golden brown. Drain on paper towels and keep warm.

Cut the anchovies to the same length as the sage leaves. Lay each anchovy on top of a sage leaf and crush gently with a fork, being careful not to tear leaves. Sandwich with another leaf, face down. Press together to seal. Fry for 1 minute on each side and drain on paper towels. Serve the escalopes with the anchovies and a good squeeze of lemon.

Serves 4

grilled sirloin with porcini cream

see variations page 200

An Italian special is a good steak with a rich porcini cream, but cream sauces can get quite rich. That's the great thing about eating tapas — the serving size means you can have a little bit of something decadent. It doesn't get much more decadent than this.

1/2 oz. dried porcini mushrooms
1/2 lb. sirloin steak
sea salt and freshly ground black pepper
3 tbsp. (3/8 stick) butter
2 shallots, finely sliced

1 clove garlic, crushed
1/2 cup homemade chicken or beef stock
1/2 tbsp. chopped fresh tarragon
2/3 cup heavy cream

Cover the porcini with hot (not boiling) water, and set aside for 20 minutes. Remove and chop the porcini and reserve the liquid. Season the steak well with salt and pepper on both sides and place onto a very hot griddle or barbecue grill for 2–3 minutes per side until charred on the outside and cooked medium-rare. Cover and set aside to rest.

Melt the butter in a small skillet and fry the shallots until soft. Add the garlic and continue to cook, stirring, for a few minutes. Add the mushrooms and fry for several minutes more. Add the mushroom soaking liquid, stock, and tarragon to the pan. Let simmer until reduced by two-thirds, then add the cream. Season and then allow the sauce to gently simmer for a few minutes before serving it over the sliced steak.

Serves 4

hanger steak with celeriac & red cabbage

see variations page 201

Another underused cut of meat is the hanger steak, which is very lean and tender. It becomes a good wintry tapas when paired with celeriac and red cabbage.

1/2 lb. celeriac
2 1/4 cups whole milk
7 tbsp. (7/8 stick) butter
sea salt and freshly ground black pepper
1 tbsp. fennel seeds, lightly pounded in a
    mortar and pestle
1 red onion, thinly sliced

1/2 lb. red cabbage, outer leaves and core
    removed, sliced thin
3 1/2 tbsp. red wine vinegar
1 tbsp. brown sugar
7 tbsp. water
1/2 lb. hanger steak
olive oil

Peel the celeriac and cut into small chunks, then gently boil it in the milk with some salt until tender. Drain well, setting aside 3 tablespoons of the milk. Put celeriac in a blender. Add half the butter, some salt and pepper, and the reserved milk. Blend to a thick puree. Keep warm. In a heavy-bottomed saucepan, melt the remaining butter on high heat. Add the fennel seeds, followed by the red onion and cabbage. Pan-fry for 5 minutes, then add the vinegar and sugar and allow it to simmer until the liquid has evaporated. Add the water and let it cook slowly for 15 minutes. Meanwhile, rub the steak all over with a little olive oil and season with salt and pepper. Heat a griddle pan or barbecue grill to high heat. When the pan is hot, cook the steak for 2–3 minutes on each side for medium-rare. Remove and set aside to rest, covered, for 10 minutes. To serve, carve the steak into 4 pieces. Spoon the celeriac puree and a spoonful of cabbage onto a plate, then top with the steak and its juices.

Serves 4

beef carpaccio with anchovy mayo & crispy garlic

see base recipe page 177

beef carpaccio with parmesan, anchovy mayo & crispy garlic
Prepare the basic recipe, adding 2 tablespoons freshly grated Parmesan
cheese to the mayonnaise and 2 tablespoons shaved Parmesan cheese on
top as a garnish.

classic beef carpaccio
Prepare the basic recipe, but omit the mayonnaise and drizzle with really good
olive oil and a squeeze of lemon juice instead. Shave 2 tablespoons Parmesan
cheese on top.

beef carpaccio with parmesan, bacon, anchovy mayo & crispy garlic
Prepare the basic recipe, adding 3 ounces crisply fried and crumbled bacon and
2 tablespoons shaved Parmesan cheese as a garnish.

beef carpaccio with anchovies, anchovy mayo & crispy garlic
Prepare the basic recipe, garnishing with an additional 12 marinated
(pickled) anchovies.

variations

beef tenderloin with rioja & blue cheese

see base recipe page 179

beef tenderloin with blue cheese
Prepare the basic recipe, omitting the red wine reduction altogether.

venison tenderloin with rioja juniper sauce & blue cheese
Prepare the basic recipe, replacing the beef with venison fillet, and the
cinnamon stick with 4 smashed juniper berries and 1 bay leaf.

pork tenderloin with rioja & blue cheese
Prepare the basic recipe, replacing the beef with pork tenderloin.

venison tenderloin with rioja & goat cheese
Prepare the basic recipe, replacing the beef with venison fillet and the blue
cheese with a really strong goat cheese.

beef skewers with béarnaise sauce

see base recipe page 180

sesame beef skewers with béarnaise sauce
Prepare the basic recipe, tossing the beef cubes in 2 tablespoons sesame seeds before cooking.

herbed beef skewers with béarnaise sauce
Prepare the basic recipe, tossing the beef cubes in 1 teaspoon fresh rosemary and 1 teaspoon fresh thyme before cooking.

venison skewers with béarnaise sauce
Prepare the basic recipe, replacing the beef with venison fillet.

beef skewers with roasted garlic béarnaise sauce
Prepare the basic recipe, adding 1 head pureed roasted garlic to the béarnaise.

ribeye with peppers & polenta fries

see base recipe page 182

ribeye with pimientos de padrón & polenta fries
Prepare the basic recipe, replacing the piquillo peppers with pimientos de Padrón.

ribeye with roasted yellow peppers & polenta fries
Prepare the basic recipe, replacing the piquillo peppers with roasted yellow peppers in oil.

ribeye with piquillo peppers & goat cheese polenta fries
Prepare the basic recipe, replacing the butter in the polenta mixture with goat cheese.

ribeye with piquillo peppers & herby polenta fries
Prepare the basic recipe, adding 1 teaspoon chopped fresh thyme to the polenta mixture.

flap steak with bone marrow

see base recipe page 184

flap steak
Prepare the basic recipe, omitting the bone marrow.

flap steak & truffle
Prepare the basic recipe, omitting the bone marrow and adding a drizzle of
white truffle oil in its place.

flap steak with pancetta & bone marrow
Prepare the basic recipe, adding 3 ounces cubed pancetta with the shallots
when making the sauce.

classic flap steak with bone marrow
Prepare the basic recipe, omitting the sauce and shallots. Simply serve the
marrow and the steak.

rich oxtail stew with parsnip puree

see base recipe page 187

braised ox cheek with parsnip puree
Prepare the basic recipe, replacing the oxtail with ox cheek and cooking for 4 hours.

stout-braised oxtail with parsnip puree
Prepare the basic recipe, replacing the red wine with stout.

rich oxtail stew with potato puree
Prepare the basic recipe, replacing the parsnips with the same volume of potatoes.

rich oxtail stew with polenta
Prepare the basic recipe, replacing the parsnip puree with polenta. Mix 3/5 cup (5 1/2 ounces) instant polenta with 2 1/2 cups boiling chicken stock and cook for 3 minutes. Stir in 2 tablespoons (1/4 stick) butter and 2 tablespoons freshly grated Parmesan cheese.

variations

veal milanese with sage & anchovies

see base recipe page 188

veal milanese with egg, sage & anchovies
Prepare the basic recipe, adding a fried egg on top of each serving.

veal milanese with sage, capers & anchovies
Prepare the basic recipe, adding 2 tablespoons capers to the skillet with the anchovies and sage leaves.

veal milanese with sage & capers
Prepare the basic recipe, omitting the anchovies and adding 2 tablespoons capers to the skillet with the sage leaves.

veal milanese with sage crumb
Prepare the basic recipe, omitting the anchovies. Finely chop the sage leaves and mix them with the bread crumbs before coating the meat.

grilled sirloin with porcini cream

see base recipe page 191

grilled sirloin with wild mushroom cream
Prepare the basic recipe, replacing the dried porcini mushrooms with a selection of seasonal wild mushrooms.

grilled sirloin with mushroom & stilton cream
Prepare the basic recipe, replacing the porcini mushrooms with sliced brown cup mushrooms. Crumble in 2 ounces crumbled blue cheese as you finish making your sauce.

grilled sirloin with stilton cream sauce
Prepare the basic recipe, but omit the mushrooms. Finish the sauce with 2 ounces crumbled stilton.

grilled sirloin with vermouth & porcini cream
Prepare the basic recipe, adding 2 tablespoons dry vermouth to the cooked mushrooms and allowing to bubble up before continuing the recipe.

hanger steak with celeriac & red cabbage

see base recipe page 192

hanger steak with potato & red cabbage
Prepare the basic recipe, replacing the celeriac puree with mashed potatoes.

hanger steak with celeriac, chestnut & red cabbage
Prepare the basic recipe, adding 3 tablespoons chestnut puree to the
celeriac puree.

hanger steak with celeriac, beet & red cabbage
Prepare the basic recipe, adding 1 grated beet to the pan with the red cabbage.

hanger steak with celeriac & spiced red cabbage
Prepare the basic recipe, adding a pinch of dried red pepper flakes and
1/2 cinnamon stick when cooking the red cabbage.

tapas exóticas
game tapas

A real chance to explore some of the more

neglected ingredients, do not let unfamiliarity be

off-putting. What could be more exiting than

venison filet with creamy celeriac or buttery

sweetbreads in sherry sauce? Just explore and enjoy.

venison with port, juniper & cinnamon with celeriac puree

see variations page 219

Melt-in-the-mouth venison steak is never better complemented than with port.

generous 1/2 lb. venison steak, trimmed
sea salt and freshly ground black pepper
2 tbsp. (1/4 stick) butter
2 tbsp. olive oil
2 sprigs fresh thyme
4 juniper berries, smashed
2 cloves garlic, roughly crushed

7 tbsp. port
scant 1 cup homemade beef stock
1 stick cinnamon
1 3/4 cups milk
9 oz. celeriac, peeled and cubed
dash red wine vinegar

Season the venison generously all over with salt and freshly ground black pepper. In a heavy skillet over medium heat, heat oil and half the butter. Fry the venison for 2–3 minutes until browned on all sides. Add the thyme, juniper berries, and garlic to the pan, and cook on low heat for 10 minutes for medium-rare. Remove the venison from the pan, set aside, and cover to rest for 10 minutes. Deglaze the skillet with the port, then add the beef stock and cinnamon, and gently reduce over medium heat. Meanwhile, season the milk well with salt and pepper and gently poach the celeriac until tender. Drain the celeriac, reserving the cooking liquid. Add the celeriac and the remaining butter to a blender with a splash of the cooking liquid and blend until completely smooth. Add a dash of vinegar to the port sauce to sharpen the flavor. Remove the cinnamon and juniper berries. Slice the venison into 4 pieces and serve on a bed of celeriac puree with a liberal drizzling of port reduction.

Serves 4

quail with pomegranate

see variations page 220

Quail with a Middle Eastern influence, coated in five-spice powder and finished in piquant pomegranate molasses and seeds.

2 medium quail (about 5 oz. each)
1 tbsp. five-spice powder
sea salt and freshly ground black pepper
good drizzle of olive oil, plus 1 tbsp.

2 tbsp. pomegranate molasses
pinch ground cinnamon
1 tbsp. pomegranate seeds

Rinse the quail under cold running water and pat dry. Rub the skins vigorously with the five-spice powder and plenty of salt and pepper, then cover and set aside for 1 hour for the flavors to really mingle with the meat.

After 1 hour, preheat the oven to 350°F. Heat a drizzle of olive oil in a large skillet over medium-high heat and add the quail, breast-side down. Cook for 3–4 minutes until lightly browned, then transfer to a roasting pan, breasts facing up. Finish cooking in the oven for 6–8 minutes. To test that the meat is juicy but not raw, insert a skewer into the thickest part of the breast. If the liquid runs clear, remove from the heat and keep warm while resting.

Meanwhile, heat the pomegranate molasses, 1 tablespoon olive oil, and cinnamon in a small saucepan. Carve the quails into quarters, removing and discarding the backbone. Serve the quail pieces on a platter, drizzled with a little pomegranate sauce and a sprinkling of pomegranate seeds.

Serves 4

roasted pheasant en cassoulet

see variations page 221

The classic cassoulet is slow-cooked beans with duck and Toulouse sausages, but there is no reason not to be slightly creative with the term. Here, we have a rich bean cassoulet topped with perfectly cooked pheasant and seasoned crumbs.

1 young plump-breasted pheasant, skin on
sea salt and freshly ground black pepper
4 tbsp. olive oil, plus extra for topping
1 small onion, finely chopped
scant 1/2 lb. cubed bacon
1 3/4 cups dry white wine
1 3/4 cups homemade chicken stock
1 bay leaf, bruised

3 sprigs fresh thyme
1 (14-oz.) can cannellini beans, rinsed and
drained
zest and juice of 1/2 small lemon
1 cup fresh white bread crumbs
1 tsp. chopped fresh parsley
1 tsp. butter, melted

Heat the oven to 350°F. Pat dry the pheasant's skin with paper towels and rub all over with salt and pepper.

In a large, heavy Dutch oven, heat 2 tablespoons oil until very hot, then brown the pheasant on all sides. Remove the bird and set aside. Lower the heat to medium. In the remaining oil, fry the onion and bacon until the onion is soft and the bacon cubes are lightly golden. Pour in the wine and let it bubble down for 1 minute to burn away the alcohol. Give the mixture a good stir to scrape up any pheasant scraps stuck to the bottom of the pan, then add the chicken stock, bay leaf, thyme, beans, and lemon zest and juice. Season with salt and pepper and mix well.

Meanwhile, mix together the crumbs, parsley, butter, and a little olive oil. Return the pheasant to the pot, pushing it down till halfway submerged in the cassoulet. Sprinkle with the crumb mixture and cook in the oven for 10 minutes. Remove the lid and cook, uncovered, for a further 10 minutes until the pheasant juices run clear when poked with a skewer. Serve right from the oven, in the Dutch oven, with everyone just grabbing a fork and digging in.

Serves 4

wild boar with wild mushrooms

see variations page 222

Wild boar has a much gamier flavor than pork, but it still feels like you're eating the same beast. So for game novices, this is the one to start with. As in the theory that what goes together grows together, I always imagine wild boars snuffling at wild mushrooms, thus making the perfect pairing.

4 cloves garlic, crushed
4 tbsp. olive oil
2 shallots, finely chopped
1/2 celery stalk, finely chopped
2 fresh bay leaves, bruised
1 sprig fresh rosemary, chopped
2 sprigs fresh thyme, chopped
4 juniper berries, lightly pounded in a
    pestle and mortar
3/4 cup red wine

sea salt and freshly ground black pepper
generous 1/2 lb. wild boar shoulder, diced
1 tbsp. flour
1 1/4 cups homemade chicken stock
2 tbsp. (1 oz.) canned chestnuts, roughly
    chopped
2 tbsp. (1/4 stick) butter
10 oz. wild mushrooms
2 tbsp. light cream

In a large bowl, make a marinade for the meat by mixing the garlic, 3 tablespoons olive oil, shallots, celery, fresh herbs, juniper berries, half the wine, and salt and pepper. Whisk well until the marinade has emulsified. Add the boar meat and toss to make sure it is evenly coated. Cover the bowl with plastic wrap and place in the refrigerator overnight.

Preheat the oven to 300°F. Over high heat, heat a Dutch oven and add the remaining tablespoon of oil. Remove the meat from the marinade and brown it well in the hot oil. Set meat aside, add the flour to the pot, and cook for 1 minute. Add the reserved marinade and cook until softened and the vegetables are beginning to caramelize. Return the meat to the

pot along with the stock and chestnuts. Bring to a boil, cover, and place in the oven for 2 1/2 hours.

Just before serving, melt the butter in a skillet and fry the mushrooms for 4–5 minutes or until brown. Stir into the casserole with the cream and serve right away with crusty bread.

Serves 4

ballotine of rabbit & white beans

see variations page 223

Normally to make a ballotine — a boned and rolled joint — is considered a little bit tricky. So get your butcher to do the hard work of boning the meat, leaving you the easy task of stuffing and rolling. The result is fantastic juicy meat with aromatic stuffing.

3 sprigs fresh rosemary, plus extra for the beans
1 whole rabbit, deboned and in 1 piece
4 sprigs fresh thyme, leaves stripped
1/3 lb. chopped lean pancetta slices
sea salt and freshly ground black pepper

2 tbsp. olive oil
1/3 lb. pancetta cubes
3/4 cup dry white wine
7 tbsp. homemade chicken stock
1 (14–oz.) can cannellini beans, drained

Lay the rabbit on a working surface, skin-side down, and spread the herbs and chopped pancetta slices along the length of the breast at one end. Sprinkle with salt and pepper. To make the ballotine, fold the breast over the stuffing and roll up tightly in plastic wrap, twisting the sides securely. Bring a large pan of water to a boil, put the wrapped ballotine in the water, and simmer for 25 minutes to poach. Remove, set aside, and let cool slightly Unwrap the ballotine. Heat a medium-sized skillet over medium to high heat, add 1 tablespoon olive oil, and fry the ballotine until golden all over. This will take about 5 minutes. Remove from the pan and let it rest. Meanwhile, in a medium saucepan, heat the remaining oil and fry the pancetta cubes until golden. Add the wine and allow to reduce by two-thirds. Pour in the chicken stock, 2 halved rosemary sprigs, and cannellini beans. Let cook on medium heat for 10 minutes, stirring gently now and again, being careful not to break up the beans. Slice the rabbit ballotine into 8 thin rounds. Serve the slices with any juices on top of the hot beans.

Serves 4

chicken livers with pedro ximénez & iberico ham

see variations page 224

Pedro Ximénez is a really thick, syrupy sweet sherry. Chicken livers are balanced perfectly by this sweetness, and this finished dish is all pulled together by the crisp saltiness of the Iberico ham (dry-cured Spanish ham).

2 tbsp. (1/4 stick) butter
1 tbsp. olive oil
4 thin slices Iberico ham

sea salt and freshly ground black pepper
3 oz. fresh chicken livers, fat removed
1/3 cup Pedro Ximénez sherry

Heat the butter and oil in a large heavy pan until really hot and the butter is foaming. Fry the ham quickly for 1 minute, until it begins to crisp up. Remove with a slotted spoon and set aside. Season the chicken livers well and cook for 30 seconds on each side. Remove from the heat and cover to keep warm. Add the Pedro Ximénez to the pan and reduce by two-thirds.

Pile the livers on a plate and top with the crisp ham. Serve drizzled with a few spoonfuls of the sherry reduction.

Serves 4

calf's liver with baby onions, serrano & sweet sherry

see variations page 225

This Spanish and much finer version of the classic liver with bacon and onions is enriched with sweet sherry, which makes it the most delicious way to serve calf's liver.

2 tbsp. (1/4 stick) butter
4 baby onions or small shallots, peeled and
    halved
3/4 cup sweet sherry
sea salt and freshly ground black pepper

4 slices Serrano ham
4 oz. calf's liver
2 tbsp. generously seasoned flour
2 tbsp. olive oil

In a medium, heavy saucepan, melt the butter and fry the onions or shallots until golden all over. Add the sherry, season with salt and pepper, and reduce the heat to a medium simmer. Allow the onions to cook in the slowly reducing sherry until tender and the liquid is a thin syrup. Broil the ham slices until they begin to crisp at the edges. Set aside and keep warm. Season the liver on both sides with salt and pepper and then coat lightly in the seasoned flour, shaking off any excess. Heat the oil in a large, heavy skillet. Add the liver and cook over high heat for 2 minutes on each side. Remove it from the pan when the liver is browned on the outside, but still pink and juicy on the inside. Slice the liver and serve with the onions and sherry reduction. Top with a scattering of bits of the crispy ham.

Serves 4

seared foie gras with sherry-soaked raisins & sourdough toasts

see variations page 226

Pan-fried foie gras is fairly opulent, but for those who love it, it's worth every penny. The sweet and boozy raisins make a wonderful pairing for the creamy foie. Enjoy.

2 tbsp. raisins

3 1/2 tbsp. sherry

2 slices raw foie gras, veins removed (best sliced with a hot knife)

sea salt and freshly ground black pepper

4 small slices sourdough bread, toasted

In a bowl, mix the raisins and sherry, cover, and set aside for at least 4 hours until the raisins have swollen up and are plump.

Heat a large nonstick skillet to very hot, and add the slices of foie gras, cooking for 40–50 seconds per side for medium-rare. Remove and place momentarily on paper towels to soak up excess fat, then move to a new plate and sprinkle with salt and pepper. Pour the raisins and excess sherry into the hot pan and with a spoon scrape up the fatty residue to make a sticky sauce.

Divide the foie gras between the toasted sourdough, top with a few soaked raisins and a drizzle of sauce, and serve immediately.

Serves 4

sweetbreads with pedro ximénez

see variations page 227

These sweetbreads are magnificent coated in the sticky king of sherries — Pedro Ximénez — and veal jus. Eating sweetbreads when dining out is really trendy, but few realize quite how easy it is to cook them at home.

1 tsp. vegetable oil
1 small carrot, roughly chopped
1 onion, chopped
1 clove garlic, crushed
1 bay leaf, bruised

5 oz. veal sweetbreads
2 tbsp. flour seasoned with salt and pepper
2 tbsp. (1/4 stick) butter
3 1/2 tbsp. Pedro Ximénez sherry
2/3 cup homemade beef stock or veal jus

Place the oil, vegetables, garlic, and bay leaf in a medium saucepan. Add the sweetbreads. Fill the pan with cold water and bring to a boil. Once the water is at boiling point, lower the temperature and simmer for 6 minutes. Remove the sweetbreads from the water and allow to cool. When cool enough to handle, peel the membrane from the sweetbreads and discard. Dredge the sweetbreads in flour, shaking off any excess, then fry in the butter for 4 minutes until golden on the outside and firm. Remove from the pan and set aside, covered, to keep warm.

Pour the Pedro Ximénez and beef stock into the pan and stir until reduced by half. To serve, toss the sweetbreads with the Pedro Ximénez sauce to evenly coat them and pile them on a platter.

Serves 4

variations

venison with port, juniper & cinnamon with celeriac puree

see base recipe page 203

venison with port, juniper & cinnamon with pomme puree
Prepare the basic recipe, but replace the celeriac with floury potatoes (like russets) to make a pomme puree.

venison with port, juniper & cinnamon with butternut squash puree
Prepare the basic recipe, but replace the celeriac with butternut squash. Instead of cooking in the milk, rub squash with some olive oil and roast in a hot oven for 25 minutes. Puree the squash with butter, salt, and pepper to serve.

venison with port, juniper, blackberries & cinnamon with celeriac puree
Prepare the basic recipe, adding 2 ounces fresh blackberries to the sauce for the last 2 minutes of cooking.

venison with port, juniper, cherries & star anise with celeriac puree
Prepare the basic recipe, replacing the cinnamon stick with 1 star anise. Add 2 ounces fresh cherries to the sauce for the last 2 minutes of cooking.

variations

quail with pomegranate

see base recipe page 205

quail with orange & pomegranate
Prepare the basic recipe, adding 2 tablespoons orange juice with
the pomegranate molasses and reducing for 1 minute.

quail with orange
Prepare the basic recipe, replacing the pomegranate molasses with
4 tablespoons orange juice, and reduce the sauce for 1 minute.
Replace the pomegranate seeds with segments of 1 orange.

duck with pomegranate
Prepare the basic recipe, replacing the quail with duck breasts. Cook
until medium-rare.

quail with pomegranate & walnuts
Prepare the basic recipe, adding 1 tablespoon chopped caramelized
walnuts, scattered over the quail.

roasted pheasant en cassoulet

see base recipe page 206

spiced roasted pheasant en cassoulet
Prepare the basic recipe, adding a pinch of dried red pepper flakes and smoked paprika for the last minute of frying the onions and bacon.

roasted pheasant en cassoulet with chorizo
Prepare the basic recipe, replacing the bacon with chopped semidry chorizo.

roasted chicken en cassoulet
Prepare the basic recipe, replacing the pheasant with chicken and cooking for 5 minutes longer.

roasted pheasant & toulouse sausage en cassoulet
Prepare the basic recipe, adding 1 garlic Toulouse sausage when browning the pheasant. Lay the sausage alongside the bird when baking in the oven.

variations

wild boar with wild mushrooms

see base recipe page 208

venison with wild mushrooms
Prepare the basic recipe, replacing the wild boar with venison shoulder.

wild boar casserole
Prepare the basic recipe, omitting the cream and mushrooms for a simpler, less rich casserole.

wild boar with apples
Prepare the basic recipe, omitting the mushrooms and adding 1 apple, cut into eighths.

wild boar with garlic & herb wild mushrooms
Prepare the basic recipe, but fry the mushrooms with 2 garlic cloves and finish with 1 teaspoon chopped fresh parsley.

variations

ballotine of rabbit & white beans

see base recipe page 210

ballotine of guinea fowl with white beans
Prepare the basic recipe, replacing the rabbit with 1 whole, boned guinea fowl.

ballotine of rabbit with lentils
Prepare the basic recipe, replacing the beans with canned green lentils.

ballotine of rabbit with white beans, rosemary & chorizo
Prepare the basic recipe, replacing the pancetta with the same quantity of semidry chorizo.

ballotine of rabbit with white beans, rosemary, pancetta & sausage
Prepare the basic recipe, adding 1/3 pound ground sausage to the herb and pancetta stuffing.

variations

chicken livers with pedro ximénez & iberico ham

see base recipe page 213

chicken livers with pedro ximénez & chorizo
Prepare the basic recipe, replacing the ham with dried sliced chorizo.

chicken livers with madeira & iberico ham
Prepare the basic recipe, replacing Pedro Ximénez with Madeira wine.

chicken livers with pedro ximénez & chestnuts
Prepare the basic recipe, omitting the ham and adding 8 peeled chestnuts.

chicken livers with pedro ximénez & sage
Prepare the basic recipe, omitting the ham and adding 8 fresh sage leaves.

chicken livers with port & pancetta
Prepare the basic recipe, replacing the ham with 1/4 cup cubed pancetta and the Pedro Ximénez with 1/3 cup port.

calf's liver with baby onions, serrano & sweet sherry

see base recipe page 214

calf's liver with baby onions, serrano, sage & sweet sherry
Prepare the basic recipe, adding 8 fresh sage leaves. Before frying the onions, fry the sage until crisp in the butter, remove with a slotted spoon, and set aside. Garnish the finished dish with the crispy sage leaves.

calf's liver with onions, serrano & sweet sherry
Prepare the basic recipe, replacing the baby onions or shallots with 1 sliced medium onion and 2 chopped fresh sage leaves, cooked down until caramelized.

calf's liver with baby onions, pancetta & sweet sherry
Prepare the basic recipe, replacing the Serrano ham with 6 slices pancetta.

calf's liver with baby onions, serrano & sweet sherry jus
Prepare the basic recipe, adding 3/4 cup homemade beef stock along with the sweet sherry to make more of a gravy.

variations

seared foie gras with sherry-soaked raisins & sourdough toasts

see base recipe page 217

seared foie gras with sherry-soaked raisins & raisin-walnut toasts
Prepare the basic recipe, replacing the sourdough with raisin-walnut bread.

seared foie gras with sherry-soaked raisins, truffle & sourdough toasts
Prepare the basic recipe, adding to the finished dish a grating of 1/4 medium white truffle or a drizzling of a small amount of white truffle oil.

seared foie gras with sherry-soaked raisins, pickled walnuts & sourdough toasts
Prepare the basic recipe, adding 1 tablespoon chopped pickled walnuts to the raisins while they are soaking.

seared foie gras with grapes & sourdough toasts
Prepare the basic recipe, replacing the raisins with seedless grapes.

variations

sweetbreads with pedro ximénez

see base recipe page 218

sweetbreads with pedro ximénez & cream
Prepare the basic recipe, adding 1 tablespoon heavy cream to the finished sauce.

sweetbreads with wild mushrooms & pedro ximénez
Prepare the basic recipe, adding 3 ounces wild mushrooms to the skillet after you have fried the sweetbreads and before you have made the sauce. Remove with a slotted spoon, then return them to the pan at the end of cooking.

sweetbreads with wild mushrooms, pedro ximénez & cream
Prepare the basic recipe, adding 3 ounces wild mushrooms to the skillet after you have fried the sweetbreads and before you have made the sauce. Remove with a slotted spoon, then add them to the pan at the end of cooking with 1 tablespoon heavy cream and a few sprigs of fresh tarragon.

sweetbreads with pancetta & pedro ximénez
Prepare the basic recipe, adding 3 ounces sliced and chopped pancetta to the skillet after you have fried the sweetbreads and before you have made the sauce. Remove with a slotted spoon, then return to the pan at the end of cooking.

tapas de vegetales

vegetable tapas

From hearty slices of traditional mini tortilla to fresh salads of exotic ingredients, vegetable dishes are a staple of all tapas. Served hot and cold, the elegant flavors speak for themselves.

patatas bravas

see variations page 246

Patatas bravas simply translates as brave potatoes. They are sliced fried potatoes smothered in a rich tomato sauce with a hint of smoky spiciness.

about 1 lb. waxy potatoes (such as Yukon Gold),
    well scrubbed
about 2 cups mild olive oil or sunflower oil for
    deep-frying
for the tomato sauce
3 tbsp. olive oil
1 small onion
1 clove garlic, peeled

1 small dried red chile
1/2 tsp. smoked paprika
4 large ripe plum tomatoes, chopped
2 tsp. tomato paste
1/2 cup water
sea salt and freshly ground black pepper
fresh flat-leaf parsley, to garnish (optional)

Cut the potatoes into even-sized chunks. Add them to a large pan half-filled with the oil and heat gently over a low flame until small bubbles rise to the surface. Cook the potatoes like this — almost poaching them in the oil — for around 12–15 minutes, until they are just tender. Then, increase the heat and deep-fry the potato pieces until golden brown.

While the potatoes are cooking, prepare the sauce. Heat the oil in a small saucepan. Finely chop the onion, garlic, and chile, and gently fry in the hot oil for 3–4 minutes, until softened but not colored. Stir in the paprika and cook for a few seconds more. Add the tomatoes to the pan. Stir in the tomato paste and water. Cook over low heat for about 10 minutes until the tomatoes are well softened, stirring occasionally. Season to taste with salt and pepper. Lift the potatoes out of the oil with a slotted spoon and drain on paper towels. Put into a warmed dish, add the tomato sauce, and serve.

Serves 4

mini tortilla

see variations page 247

The great thing about doing a small tortilla is that it feeds 4 in a tapas portion perfectly, but also allows the dish to be slightly underdone, meaning a gooey middle.

1 medium potato (such as a Yukon Gold),
   thinly sliced
1 cup olive oil
1 onion, thinly sliced

2 large free-range eggs
1 free-range egg yolk
sea salt and freshly ground black pepper

Place the potato slices in a small pan and add all except 1 tablespoon of the oil. Gently heat until the potatoes are just tender, about 8 minutes. Remove from the pan and let cool. In a small pan, heat the remaining olive oil over low heat. Add the sliced onions and fry very slowly for 10–15 minutes until they have really softened and started to turn golden. Remove from the pan and let cool. Mix the potato, eggs, and egg yolk thoroughly, and season with salt and pepper. Add the onions before pouring the whole lot into a small skillet, preferably about 4 inches in diameter. Turn the heat down to its lowest setting immediately.

Every now and then, draw the edge in gently with a spatula, as this will give it a lovely rounded edge. When it is firm and sealed on the outside but still a little gooey in the middle, turn it over to cook the other side. To do this, place a flat lid or plate over the pan and carefully invert both so that the omelet is on the lid or plate. Put the pan back on the heat and use the spatula to gently ease the omelet back in. Give it about 2 minutes more, then turn the heat off and leave it for a further 5 minutes to settle. It should then be cooked through but still moist, even a bit runny in the center.

Serves 4

zucchini flowers stuffed with goat cheese & lavender honey

see variations page 248

When small zucchini flower in summer, they are a treat to behold. They are perfect for stuffing and require little time to cook. Honey might seem a surprising ingredient in this dish, but lavender honey has a more savory flavor than most honey and beautifully complements the salty goat cheese.

vegetable oil for deep-frying
4 small zucchini with flowers attached
1/2 cup (3 1/2 oz.) soft goat cheese
zest of 1 lemon
4 tbsp. all-purpose flour

2 tbsp. cornstarch
sea salt and freshly ground black pepper
ice-cold sparkling water
1 tbsp. lavender honey

Heat the oil in a deep-fat fryer or wok to 350°F. Wipe the zucchini clean with a damp towel and then gently pry open the flower petals. Whip together the goat cheese and lemon zest and split it between the flowers. Seal the petals around the filling to encase it.

Gently mix together the flour and cornstarch with the salt and pepper. Whisk in just enough sparkling water to make a medium-thick batter (a bit thinner than a pancake batter). Plunge the zucchini and flowers into the batter to entirely coat them and then, one by one, place them into the hot oil to cook for 4–6 minutes or until the batter is crisp and golden. Scoop out and drain on paper towels. Lay on a serving plate and drizzle with the honey and more sea salt and black pepper.

Serves 4

mushrooms in garlic & herbs

see variations page 249

While the ingredients are simple the result is excellent. Garlic really brings out the flavor of mushrooms. Make sure you have plenty of bread to soak up the delicious juices.

2 tbsp. olive oil
5 cloves garlic, thinly sliced
1 lb. fresh mushrooms (a mix of varieties if you desire), cleaned and sliced

1/2 cup dry sherry
2 tbsp. chopped fresh flat-leaf parsley
sea salt and freshly ground black pepper

Heat the oil in a skillet over medium heat until hot. Add the garlic and sauté until it begins to turn golden. Add the mushrooms and cook, stirring vigorously, until golden brown. Add the dry sherry, bring to a boil, and continue to cook for 1 minute. Stir in the parsley and season with salt and pepper. Transfer to a serving dish.

Serves 4

phyllo pastry with feta & spinach

see variations page 250

The combination of ingredients for this delicious savory pastry is classic. The great news is that it works brilliantly with a whole variety of other options. You can freeze what you don't eat, or just eat the leftovers as snacks. You can also make this several hours in advance and bake it just before serving.

1/2 lb. feta cheese
1 lb. ricotta
10 oz. baby spinach, cooked and chopped
1 bunch scallions, finely sliced
1 green chile, finely chopped
1/3 cup freshly grated Parmesan

1 egg
a good grating nutmeg
1/2 cup fresh white bread crumbs
2 tbsp. olive oil
6 sheets phyllo pastry, trimmed to snugly fit
    baking pan

Heat oven to 350°F. Mash feta in a large mixing bowl, add the ricotta, and mash again to thoroughly mix. Stir in the spinach, scallions, chile, Parmesan, egg, nutmeg, and plenty of salt and pepper with half the bread crumbs.

Brush an 8 x 12-inch baking pan with a little olive oil. Layer half the phyllo sheets into the pan, brushing each with oil before adding the next. Scatter with the remaining bread crumbs.

Spoon in the ricotta filling and gently spread over the phyllo, so as not to move around the bread crumbs. Cover with the remaining phyllo, brushing with oil as you go, and finishing with a good coating of oil on top. Score into small triangular portions. Bake for 35–40 minutes until golden and crisp.

Serves 4

artichoke with spicy lemon crumbs

see variations page 251

A whole globe artichoke becomes a magical treat as you peel off the leaves, dip, and eat as you work your way to the more meaty heart. To serve this, everyone just reaches into the center of the table where you have the single artichoke on a plate and the vinaigrette in a bowl next to it — just dunk away and eat together.

1 large globe artichoke
juice and zest of 1 lemon
1/3 cup dry bread crumbs
2 tbsp. grated Parmesan cheese
pinch dried red pepper flakes
1 tbsp. assorted chopped fresh herbs
1 tbsp. olive oil

sea salt and freshly ground black pepper
for the vinaigrette
1 tsp. Dijon mustard
1 tbsp. sherry vinegar
squeeze of lemon juice
sea salt and freshly ground black pepper
3 tbsp. good Spanish olive oil

Simmer the artichoke in salted water, which has been acidulated with a good squeeze of lemon juice, for 30 minutes, or until the leaves can be removed with a slight tug. Remove the artichoke from the water. While still warm, press the leaves gently back, leaving them attached, so that the artichoke resembles a flower. Pull out the small white and purple center leaves and scrape out the choke (the fuzzy part) with a spoon. Stand the artichoke upright in a small baking dish. Preheat the oven to 350°F. Combine the bread crumbs, Parmesan, lemon zest, red pepper flakes, herbs, and oil. Season to taste with salt and pepper. Pack the mixture into the artichoke. Bake for 25 minutes or until golden. Meanwhile, make the vinaigrette by whisking together all the ingredients until thick and emulsified. To eat the artichoke, pull the leaves off, dip into the vinaigrette and scrape the soft base of the leaf off with your teeth. When you've finished the leaves, eat the rest of the heart.
Serves 4

asparagus with spinach, garlic & pine nuts

see variations page 252

A spring vegetable native to the Mediterranean, asparagus is well worth the wait for its unbeatable flavor and freshness. This dish is so simple to prepare and the combination of textures from the asparagus, spinach, and pine nuts is a treat.

1 bunch asparagus (about 12 spears)
1 tbsp. olive oil
2 cloves garlic, chopped
pinch dried red pepper flakes

1 tbsp. pine nuts
good handful baby leaf spinach
sea salt and freshly ground black pepper

Bring a pot of salted water to a boil, then plunge the asparagus in for 2 minutes. Drain and place the asparagus in ice-cold water.

Heat the oil in a skillet. Add the garlic, red pepper flakes, and pine nuts, then sauté gently for 1–2 minutes until the garlic and pine nuts turn lightly golden. Add the spinach and sauté until just wilted. Finally add the asparagus, and fry for another minute before seasoning with salt and pepper. Tumble the whole ensemble onto a plate and serve immediately.

Serves 4

celeriac truffle gratin

see variations page 253

This tasty but light dish is made all the more special when drizzled with a little truffle oil. Celeriac brings an unusual freshness of flavor to the gratin, cutting through the richness of the cream.

1 floury potato (such as russet), peeled
1/2 lb. celeriac, peeled
1/4 cup whipping cream

1 clove garlic, crushed
2 tbsp. (1/4 stick) butter
1 tsp. truffle oil

Preheat the oven to 350°F. Using a mandoline or very sharp knife, thinly slice the potato and celeriac.

Place the cream, garlic, and butter in a large heavy pan and bring to a boil. Stir in the sliced celeriac and potato to coat them in the mixture, then remove the pan from the heat. Stir in the truffle oil.

Layer the coated slices of potato and celeriac in a small, deep baking dish, pressing down as you go. Pour the remaining sauce over them. Bake for 45–60 minutes, or until tender all the way through. Serve hot.

Serves 4

grilled belgian endive with walnuts & pomegranate seeds

see variations page 254

The bitterness of Belgian endive combined with toasted walnuts and sweet pomegranate gives this dish a delightful nutty-fruity Middle Eastern feel. The best way to extract pomegranate seeds from the fruit is to cut it in half and then hit the back with a spoon. The fresh red seeds will fly out to be collected and used.

2 heads Belgian endive, halved through the
    stem
2 tbsp. extra-virgin olive oil
sea salt and freshly ground black pepper

1 tbsp. roughly chopped walnuts
2 tbsp. pomegranate molasses
2 tsp. walnut oil
1/3 cup pomegranate seeds (arils)

Heat a griddle pan until almost smoking. Rub the endive with half the olive oil, salt, and pepper. Lay the endive in the pan, cut-side down, and cook for 2 minutes, then turn over and cook for a minute on the other side. Remove and set on a serving plate.

In a separate pan, heat the remaining olive oil. Add the walnuts and toast for 1–2 minutes or until they have become toasty and golden. Remove from the heat and whisk in the molasses and walnut oil.

Pour the dressing over the endive. Top with the pomegranate seeds and serve.

Serves 4

warm lentils, goat's curd & beets

see variations page 255

This is great food eaten at its best. The creamy curd cheese slowly melts into the warm lentils, while the beets release their juices. All the flavors ooze together. If you cannot find goat's curd, a very young and soft chèvre (goat cheese) will make a fine substitute.

1/2 cup lentils du Puy (small French-style
    lentils)
2 small shallots, finely sliced
1 tomato, finely chopped
3 tbsp. extra-virgin olive oil
1 tbsp. sherry vinegar

1 tbsp. finely chopped mint
sea salt and ground black pepper
1/4 lb. goat's curd or a young, soft chèvre
1 medium beet, roasted, peeled,
    and thickly sliced

Place the lentils in a pan of boiling water. Do not add salt or this will toughen the lentils. Boil for 25 minutes or until tender. Remove, drain, and let steam off the heat for 5 minutes.

Combine the lentils, shallots, tomato, oil, vinegar, and mint. Season with salt and pepper. Set aside to marinate for another 5–10 minutes.

Place on a serving plate and top with the curd and then the sliced beet.

Serves 4

variations

patatas bravas

see base recipe page 229

patatas bravas with aïoli
Prepare the basic recipe, but serve with a garlicky aïoli (page 92) on the side in place of or along with the spicy tomato sauce.

patatas bravas with chorizo
Prepare the basic recipe, adding 6 slices sliced and fried chorizo on top of the dish.

patatas bravas with piquillo peppers
Prepare the basic recipe, adding 2 chopped piquillo peppers (jarred roasted red peppers) to the sauce at the end of cooking.

patatas bravas with blood sausage
Prepare the basic recipe, adding 1 Spanish blood sausage, chopped and fried, to the cooked potatoes just before covering with the sauce.

mini tortilla

see base recipe page 231

mini sweet potato tortilla
Prepare the basic recipe, replacing the potato with a sweet potato.

mini red pepper & potato tortilla
Prepare the basic recipe, adding 1 sliced jarred roasted red pepper to the egg mixture before cooking.

mini chorizo & potato tortilla
Prepare the basic recipe, adding 2 slices chorizo to the egg mixture before cooking.

mini spinach & potato tortilla
Prepare the basic recipe, adding 4 tablespoons cooked and drained spinach to the egg mixture before cooking.

zucchini flowers stuffed with goat cheese & lavender honey

see base recipe page 232

zucchini flowers stuffed with goat cheese & thyme honey
Prepare the basic recipe, replacing the lavender honey with thyme honey for a savory finish.

tempura asparagus with goat cheese & lavender honey
Prepare the basic recipe, replacing the zucchini with some thick asparagus sliced lengthwise in half. Stuff the asparagus with the cheese filling before sandwiching the halves together and coating with the batter.

zucchini flowers stuffed with peppered cream cheese & lavender honey
Prepare the basic recipe, replacing the goat cheese with 1/2 cup cream cheese beaten with 1/2 teaspoon of freshly ground black pepper.

variations

mushrooms in garlic & herbs

see base recipe page 234

chile & mushrooms in garlic & herbs
Prepare the basic recipe, adding 1 sliced dried chile to the skillet with
the garlic.

creamy mushrooms in garlic & herbs
Prepare the basic recipe, adding 3 tablespoons whipping cream with the
parsley at the end of cooking.

balsamic mushrooms in garlic & herbs
Prepare the basic recipe, adding 1/2 tablespoon balsamic vinegar after frying
the garlic and before adding the mushrooms.

lemon mushrooms in garlic & herbs
Prepare the basic recipe, adding the zest and juice of 1/2 lemon once the
mushrooms have been cooked and before adding the sherry.

variations

phyllo pastry with feta & spinach

see base recipe page 236

phyllo pastry with feta, spinach & lemon
Prepare the basic recipe, adding the zest and juice of 1 lemon to the filling.

phyllo pastry with feta & lemon
Prepare the basic recipe, omitting the spinach and adding the zest and juice of
1 lemon to the cheese mixture.

puff pastry with feta & spinach
Prepare the basic recipe, but instead of sandwiching between sheets of phyllo
pastry, make small turnovers, like Cornish pasties, using pieces of thinly rolled
puff pastry.

variations

artichoke with spicy lemon crumbs

see base recipe page 239

boiled artichoke with vinaigrette
Prepare the basic recipe, but omit the bread crumb stuffing. Do not bake.
To serve, fill the center with the vinaigrette.

baked artichoke with spicy preserved lemon crumbs
Prepare the basic recipe, omitting the Parmesan cheese and adding
1 chopped preserved lemon to the stuffing mix.

baked artichoke with capers & mint crumbs
Prepare the basic recipe, omitting the red pepper flakes and herbs and
adding 1 tablespoon chopped capers and 1 tablespoon chopped fresh mint
leaves to the stuffing.

boiled artichoke filled with crabmeat salad
Prepare the basic recipe, omitting the bread crumb stuffing and the
vinaigrette. After boiling and cooling the artichoke, fill it with a salad of
5 tablespoons white crabmeat, 1/2 finely chopped red chile, the juice and
zest of 1 lemon, and 1 tablespoon finely chopped cilantro.

variations

asparagus with spinach, garlic & pine nuts

see base recipe page 240

asparagus with spinach, garlic, pine nuts & lemon
Prepare the basic recipe, adding the juice of 1/2 lemon at the end of cooking. Just squeeze the lemon over the mixture before serving.

asparagus with garlic & pine nuts
Prepare the basic recipe, omitting the spinach.

asparagus with spinach, garlic & hazelnuts
Prepare the basic recipe, replacing the pine nuts with roughly chopped hazelnuts.

zucchini with spinach, garlic & pine nuts
Prepare the basic recipe, replacing the asparagus with 1/2 pound baby zucchini, sliced in half lengthwise.

celeriac truffle gratin

see base recipe page 241

potato truffle gratin
Prepare the basic recipe, replacing the celeriac with 2 more potatoes.

celeriac gratin
Prepare the basic recipe, but omit the truffle oil.

celeriac, porcini mushroom & truffle gratin
Prepare the basic recipe, adding 2 sliced and sautéed fresh porcini mushrooms. Layer them in with the celeriac and potatoes.

root vegetable gratin
Prepare the basic recipe, omitting the single potato and two-thirds of the celeriac. Use equal amounts of celeriac, parsnip, turnip, and potato. Omit the truffle oil.

grilled belgian endive with walnuts & pomegranate seeds

see base recipe page 243

grilled red endive with pine nuts & pomegranate seeds
Prepare the basic recipe, replacing the endive with 2 heads of red endive, and the walnuts with 1 tablespoon pine nuts.

grilled radicchio with walnuts & pomegranate seeds
Prepare the basic recipe, replacing the endive with 2 heads of radicchio.

grilled belgian endive with walnuts, lemon & pomegranate seeds
Prepare the basic recipe, adding the zest and juice of 1 lemon with the pomegranate molasses.

grilled belgian endive with grilled halloumi, lemon & pomegranate seeds
Prepare the basic recipe, but grill 2 slices of halloumi cheese with the endive and add the zest and juice of 1 lemon with the pomegranate molasses.

warm lentils, goat's curd & beets

see base recipe page 244

warm lentils, grilled goat cheese & beets
Prepare the basic recipe, replacing the goat's curd with 1 medium slice of grilled goat cheese.

warm lentils, smoked mackerel, goat's curd & beets
Prepare the basic recipe, adding 1/4 pound flaked smoked mackerel to the lentil salad.

warm lentils, goat's curd & roasted tomatoes
Prepare the basic recipe, replacing the beet with 2 halved and slow-roasted vine-ripened tomatoes.

warm lentils, grilled haloumi & beets
Prepare the basic recipe, replacing the goat's curd with 1 thick slice of grilled haloumi cheese.

tapas dulces
dessert tapas

Dessert tapas is a sweet free-for-all of miniature traditional Spanish desserts and completely new ideas. So to finish, indulge in tarts, dunk churros in oozy chocolate sauce or savor a smooth crème Catalana.

crème catalana

see variations page 273

Crème catalana is a pudding that's very similar to crème brûlée, but the custard base is not baked but thickened and set with a little cornstarch. It has a great depth and warmth of flavor from the lemon and cinnamon.

2/3 cup whole milk, plus an extra splash
scant 1 cup heavy cream
1/2 cinnamon stick
zest of 1 lemon

3 large free-range egg yolks
3/4 cup sugar, plus 1 tablespoon for the topping
2 tsp. cornstarch

In a heavy saucepan, mix the milk, cream, cinnamon, and lemon zest. Bring to a boil, then remove from the heat and leave for 10 minutes to cool and infuse.

Meanwhile, with an electric mixer, beat the egg yolks until pale, then whisk in 3/4 cup sugar. Strain the milk and whisk into the egg mixture. Dissolve the cornstarch in the extra splash of milk and then whisk into the milk-egg mixture.

Pour the mixture into a new pan and cook over low heat, stirring briskly, until it begins to thicken to a custard and coat the back of the spoon. Pour the custard into 4 small crème catalana dishes and let cool before covering and refrigerating.

Before serving, sprinkle the extra sugar on top and caramelize under a hot broiler or by blasting it with a cooking blowtorch.

Serves 4

rice pudding with pistachios &
pomegranate–rosewater syrup

see variations page 274

This Indian-inspired rice pudding is so special you'll be licking the saucepan.

1 tsp. butter
4 tbsp. short-grain rice, soaked in cold water
   for an hour, drained
2–3 cardamom seeds, ground
4 cups whole milk
3 tbsp. whole almonds

1/4 cup light brown sugar
1 1/4 cups pomegranate juice
1/4 tsp. rosewater
4 tbsp. chopped pistachios
crystallized rose petals, for serving
2 tbsp. pomegranate seeds, for serving

Heat the butter in a pan. Add the soaked rice and cook, stirring, for 2–3 minutes. Add the cardamom and milk and cook over a low heat, stirring every now and then, for 1 hour until the rice absorbs the milk. Pulse or process the almonds and sugar in a food processor until they are powdery, or even a bit pasty. Stir the almond paste into the rice and cook for 5 minutes. Set aside to cool in the refrigerator.

Pour the pomegranate juice into a small pan, bring to a boil, and reduce by two-thirds until syrupy. Remove from the heat, stir in the rosewater, and let cool. To serve, transfer the rice pudding into small dessert dishes (glass dishes are lovely for this) and top with a drizzle of syrup, some pistachios, rose petals, and pomegranate seeds.

Serves 4

apricot & almond tart

see variations page 275

Apricots and almonds. How Spanish is that? This Spanish tart will make too many slices for tapas, but the scraps will get gobbled up in no time. Delicious with whipped cream.

for the pastry
1 1/2 cups all-purpose flour
1/2 cup (1 stick) unsalted butter, cold and diced
pinch sea salt
1/4 cup granulated sugar
2 free-range eggs
for the filling
3 heaping tbsp. apricot jam
8 apricots, halved and pitted

10 tbsp. (1 1/4 sticks) unsalted butter
3/4 cup granulated sugar
3 large free-range eggs, beaten
1 free-range egg yolk
1 cup ground almonds
zest of 1 lemon
1 tsp. vanilla extract
1 tbsp. slivered almonds
confectioners' sugar, for dusting

To make the pastry, put the flour, butter, salt, and sugar in a food processor. Process until the mixture resembles bread crumbs. Add 1 egg and pulse until the dough comes together. If it is too dry, add 1–2 teaspoons of ice-cold water. Flatten the dough into a circle, cover with plastic wrap, and chill for 30 minutes.

Roll out the pastry on a lightly floured surface to about 1/8-inch thickness. Line an 8-inch, 1 1/2-inch-deep fluted tart pan. Prick the pastry base with a fork and chill for 20 minutes. Heat the oven to 350°F. Line the pastry shell with baking parchment and fill with pie weights. Cook for about 20 minutes until the pastry is a pale golden color. Take out the pie weights, brush the inside of the pastry with a beaten egg, and cook for another 5 minutes. Remove and cool slightly.

Spread the apricot jam in an even layer over the base of the pastry shell. Lay the apricot halves over the top, cut-side down. Mix the butter and sugar. Gradually add the beaten eggs and egg yolk. Fold in the ground almonds, lemon zest, and vanilla extract. Spoon the mixture over the jam and spread level. Scatter with the slivered almonds and bake for 25–30 minutes until golden and set. Serve warm or cool with a dusting of confectioners' sugar.

Makes 8–10 slices

natas

see variations page 276

Natas, the famous Portuguese custard tarts, are one of the tastiest pastries on the planet. You can find them in bakeries and delis, but try making them yourself and wow your loved ones.

2/3 cup whole milk
1/4 cup heavy cream
2 large free-range egg yolks
2 tbsp. light brown sugar
pinch salt

1 tbsp. cornstarch
1/2 cinnamon stick
1/2 vanilla bean, seeded
1 sheet (1/2 lb.) puff pastry
1 tbsp. confectioners' sugar

In a large, heavy saucepan, combine milk, cream, egg yolks, sugar, salt, and cornstarch. Mix well until all the ingredients are smoothly combined, then add the cinnamon stick and vanilla pod and seeds. Turn on the heat to low, and stir continuously with a wooden spoon. Slowly the mixture should become thicker and hold to the back of the spoon. At this point, when it resembles a thin custard, remove it from the heat, cover, and let cool completely. Meanwhile, preheat the oven to 350°F. Roll up the puff pastry into a tight roll. Slice into 3/4-inch pieces and then roll each out into a flat round. Quickly, with your thumbs, work the rounds into the cups of a nonstick regular (12-cup) muffin pan and gently press to the sides of each cup. When the pastry shells are ready, fill them two-thirds full with the custard (do not fill to the top) and dust each one with confectioners' sugar. Place the muffin pan in the oven and bake for 20 minutes until the pastry is golden and the custard is set with a slight wobble. Let the tarts cool in the muffin pan. Serve cold as a tapas dessert and save the rest for a snack with a cup of coffee.

Makes about 8 tarts

churros con chocolade

see variations page 277

Churros are sausage-shaped donuts that are meant for plunging in the thick chocolate sauce served with them. They're a tradition all day and are also eaten for breakfast.

2/3 cup water
4 tbsp. vegetable oil, plus more for deep-frying
1/2 cup flour
pinch of salt

2 free-range eggs
1/4 cup granulated sugar
2 oz. chocolate
2/3 cup heavy cream

Place the water in a saucepan with 4 tablespoons oil and bring to a boil. Mix the flour with the salt and gradually add it to the boiling water. Stir well with a wooden spoon over low heat until the mixture sticks together and leaves the sides of the pan. Remove from the heat and then beat in the eggs.

Add enough vegetable oil to a large, heavy saucepan to come halfway up the sides, and heat it to 350°F. Spoon the churros mixture into a pastry bag fitted with a large star-shaped tip. Pipe 3– or 4–inch lengths of dough directly into the hot oil and cook for 3 minutes until crisp and golden. Spoon the churros onto a plate lined with paper towels and sprinkle with the granulated sugar. Repeat until all the churros mixture is used up.

To make the chocolate dip, gently warm the chocolate and cream together in a small saucepan. When the mixture is smooth, remove it from the heat and transfer to a small bowl. Serve with a pile of the hot churros.

Serves 4

panna cotta with roasted rhubarb

see variations page 278

Panna cotta is Italian for "cooked cream," a simple eggless custard. This version is much lighter, with a yogurty tang. It is set with gelatin and served with piquant roast rhubarb.

1/2 oz. (2 packages) unflavored gelatin
1 cup cold whole milk
zest of 1 orange
2 vanilla beans, split
3/4 cup light brown sugar
1/3 cup whipping cream

1 2/3 cups Greek yogurt
for the rhubarb
1 lb. fresh rhubarb
4 tbsp. light brown sugar
1 tbsp. grenadine
2 tbsp. ginger syrup

Place the gelatin in a small bowl with 6 tablespoons of the cold milk and let stand for 5 minutes. Place the bowl in a pan of almost simmering water, stirring until all the gelatin granules are dissolved. Do not let the gelatin boil.

Place the orange zest, vanilla beans, and sugar in a pan. Add the remaining milk and cream, then bring to a boil. Turn off the heat. Strain the gelatin mixture into the hot milk mixture, stirring until completely mixed in. Very slowly whisk this into the Greek yogurt (by pouring the thin milk mixture into the thick yogurt, you'll keep it from becoming lumpy). Pour through a sieve, then pour into 4 molds. Cover each mold with plastic wrap, then chill for about 5 hours.

While the panna cotta is setting, roast the rhubarb. Preheat the oven to 400°F. Slice the rhubarb into 3/4-inch chunks and scatter in a baking pan. Sprinkle with sugar, then pour the

grenadine and ginger syrup over the rhubarb. Cover with foil and bake for 10–12 minutes or until just cooked. Let cool.

Take the panna cotta out of the refrigerator, slide a knife around the edge of each mold, and dip very briefly in hot water to loosen. Tip the panna cotta into the middle of a plate, then arrange the rhubarb pieces around it. Spoon the rhubarb sauce over the top and serve.

Serves 4

chocolate lava cake

see variations page 279

The best lava cake recipe you will find. Serve with pistachio ice cream for a bit of Mediterranean flair.

4 oz. dark chocolate (70% cocoa solids)
4 free-range eggs
3/4 cup confectioners' sugar
1/2 cup (1 stick) butter, melted

1/3 cup flour
2–3 tbsp. Cognac XO
pistachio ice cream, for serving

Melt the chocolate gently in a bowl set over a pan of simmering water. In a separate bowl, with an electric whisk, whisk together the eggs and sugar until light and fluffy and doubled in volume. Stir the melted butter into the chocolate, then fold the chocolate into the egg mixture. Whisk in the flour and add the cognac to taste (about 3 tablespoons). Chill for several hours.

Heat the oven to 400°F. Butter and flour 4 3-inch metal molds or ramekins.

Spoon the mixture into the molds (there might be a little left over) and bake for 8–10 minutes or until just firm on top. Turn out onto individual plates and serve immediately or you won't have a sauce in the center. Serve with pistachio ice cream.

Serves 4

orange custard tart

see variations page 280

An orange and nutmeg tart with sufficient orangey wobble.

1 sheet refrigerated pastry
1 whole nutmeg, for grating
4 large free-range eggs
3/4 cup light brown sugar

finely grated zest of 1 orange
1 1/4 cups whipping cream
1 1/4 cups whole milk
1 vanilla bean, seeds scraped out

Preheat the oven to 400°F. Roll out the pastry about 1/2 inch thick, then, using a fine grater, grate a dusting of nutmeg over the pastry. Fold the dough in half, then roll out again, to 1/4-inch thickness and large enough to line an 8-inch loose-bottomed tart pan with some overhang. Press the pastry into the pan (leave the excess draped over the sides), put onto a baking sheet, and chill for 10 minutes. Line the pastry with baking parchment and fill with pie weights. Bake for 20 minutes, then remove weights and paper. Bake for another 15 minutes until golden. Remove from the oven and trim the tart's overhanging edges with a sharp serrated knife. Leave the tart in the pan and set aside.

Turn the oven down to 300°F. Whisk together the eggs and sugar in a large bowl. Put a few good gratings of nutmeg, the orange zest, cream, milk, and vanilla bean and seeds into a saucepan. Bring to a boil, then pour the hot mixture onto the eggs, whisking continuously. Strain the mixture into a large measuring cup. Put the tart pan onto the pulled-out oven rack, then pour the custard into the tart shell. You may not need every last drop. Grate with a nice generous layer of nutmeg, then slide gently back into the oven and bake for 1 hour. When it's ready, the tart should be set and pale golden on the top, and have just the merest tremor in the center when you jiggle the pan. Cool, then serve in slices.

Makes 8–10 slices

turron

see variations page 281

Turron is the Spanish version of halva. It sticks to your teeth when you eat it but crumbles when you handle it. More like a candy than a dessert, it's essential alongside a dark cup of coffee.

1 cup orange blossom honey	pinch ground cinnamon
1 1/2 cups finely ground almonds	zest of 1/2 lemon
2 free-range egg yolks	1 egg white, stiffly beaten

Pour the honey into a saucepan and warm over medium-low heat to 275°F. Stir the almonds into the warm honey and remove from heat. Mix the egg yolks, cinnamon, and lemon zest into the almonds. Fold the beaten egg white into the mixture.

Line an 8-inch dish with parchment paper. Pour the mixture onto the parchment paper and smooth to a 1/2-inch layer. Place a sheet of parchment paper atop the mixture, then place a cutting board over the paper, and place a few items on top of the cutting board to give it some weight.

Allow the turron to dry for 3 days at room temperature. Cut into 1-inch squares to serve.

Makes 30 pieces

crème catalana

see base recipe page 257

vanilla crème catalana
Prepare the basic recipe, replacing the cinnamon stick with 1 vanilla bean, seeded. Add both the seeds and the bean to the milk to infuse.

orange crème catalana
Prepare the basic recipe, replacing the lemon zest with the zest of 1/2 orange.

cardamom crème catalana
Prepare the basic recipe, adding 2 crushed cardamon pods to the milk infusion.

spiced crème catalana
Prepare the basic recipe, adding 2 whole cloves, 1/2 star anise, and the zest of 1/2 orange to the infusion.

variations

rice pudding with pistachios & pomegranate-rosewater syrup

see base recipe page 259

rice pudding with pomegranate-rosewater syrup & caramelized pistachios
Prepare the basic recipe, replacing the pistachios with caramelized pistachios.

cinnamon rice pudding with pistachios & pomegranate-rosewater syrup
Prepare the basic recipe, adding 1 cinnamon stick when you start cooking the rice.

lemon rice pudding with pistachios & pomegranate-rosewater syrup
Prepare the basic recipe, adding some lemon zest when you start cooking the rice.

orange & bay rice pudding with pistachios & pomegranate syrup
Prepare the basic recipe, omitting the cardamom and adding some orange zest and 1 bay leaf. Omit the rosewater from the pomegranate sauce.

variations

apricot & almond tart

see base recipe page 260

raspberry & almond tart
Prepare the basic recipe, replacing the apricot jam and fresh apricots with raspberry jam and 1/2 pound fresh raspberries.

plum & almond tart
Prepare the basic recipe, replacing the apricot jam and fresh apricots with plum jam and fresh plums.

pear & almond tart
Prepare the basic recipe, omitting the apricot jam and replacing the fresh apricots with 8 poached and halved pears.

apricot & pistachio tart
Prepare the basic recipe, using 2/3 cup ground almonds and 1/3 cup very finely chopped pistachios.

variations

natas

see base recipe page 262

chocolate natas
Prepare the basic recipe, stirring 2 ounces melted dark chocolate into the finished custard mixture.

cardamom & rosewater natas
Prepare the basic recipe, adding 3 crushed cardamom pods and 1/4 teaspoon rosewater as you make the custard.

coffee natas
Prepare the basic recipe, adding 1 tablespoon strong black espresso to the hot custard mixture.

lemon natas
Prepare the basic recipe, adding the zest of 1/2 lemon to the hot custard.

churros con chocolade

see base recipe page 265

cinnamon churros con chocolade
Prepare the basic recipe, adding 1 teaspoon ground cinnamon to the granulated sugar.

churros con chocolade with chili powder
Prepare the basic recipe, adding a pinch of chili powder to the chocolate sauce.

churros con dulce de leche
Prepare the basic recipe, replacing the chocolate sauce with 3–4 tablespoons of dulce de leche.

churros con chocolade with orange
Prepare the basic recipe, adding the zest of 1 orange to the chocolate sauce.

panna cotta with roasted rhubarb

see base recipe page 266

panna cotta with roasted peaches
Prepare the basic recipe, omitting the grenadine, replacing the rhubarb with sliced peeled ripe peaches, and replacing the ginger syrup with 3–4 shredded fresh mint leaves.

panna cotta with gingered berries
Prepare the basic recipe, replacing the rhubarb with a mixture of fresh berries and omitting the roasting step. Mix the berries with the sugar and syrup and allow them to stand for 10 minutes to macerate.

panna cotta with roasted plums
Prepare the basic recipe, replacing the rhubarb with ripe plums.

classic panna cotta with roasted rhubarb
Prepare the basic recipe, replacing the Greek yogurt with heavy cream.

variations

chocolate lava cake

see base recipe page 269

chocolate toffee lava cake with vanilla ice cream
Prepare the basic recipe, but stuff each cake with 2 toffee candies before baking. Replace the pistachio ice cream with vanilla ice cream.

chocolate amaretto lava cake with vanilla ice cream
Prepare the basic recipe, replacing the cognac with amaretto liqueur. Replace the pistachio ice cream with vanilla ice cream.

chocolate orange lava cake
Prepare the basic recipe, adding the grated zest of 1 orange to the chocolate mixture.

chocolate raspberry lava cake with vanilla ice cream
Prepare the basic recipe, stuffing each cake with 3-4 fresh raspberries. Replace the pistachio ice cream with vanilla ice cream.

variations

orange custard tart

see base recipe page 270

orange custard tart with caramelized oranges
Prepare the basic recipe. Serve the tart with caramelized oranges. Drizzle
3 peeled and sliced oranges with a caramel sauce, made by melting 1/4 cup
sugar slowly in a dry pan and thinning it with the remaining orange juice.

custard & nutmeg tart
Prepare the basic recipe, omitting the orange zest.

lemon custard tart
Prepare the basic recipe, replacing the orange zest with the finely grated zest
of 2 lemons.

white chocolate custard tart
Prepare the basic recipe, adding 3 1/2 ounces melted and cooled white
chocolate to the base custard mixture.

variations

turron

see base recipe page 272

pistachio turron
Prepare the basic recipe, adding 1 cup pistachios after you have folded in the egg white.

whole almond turron
Prepare the basic recipe, adding 1 cup whole almonds after you have folded in the egg white.

whole almond & apricot turron
Prepare the basic recipe, adding 1/2 cup whole almonds and 1/2 cup chopped dried apricots after you have folded in the egg white.

lavender turron
Prepare the basic recipe, replacing the orange blossom honey with lavender honey.

index

A

adobo
 pork ribs in adobo
  barbecue sauce 134,
  146
almonds
 apricot & almond tart
  260, 275
 roasted almonds & seeds
  19, 33
 whole almond & apricot
  turron 281
 whole almond turron
  281
amaretto
 chocolate amaretto
  fondant with vanilla
  ice cream 279
anchovies 11
 anchovy & olive
  tapenade 44, 62
 beef carpaccio with
  anchovy mayo & crispy
  garlic 177, 193
 boquerones 24, 36
 garlic & rosemary
  marinated lamb kebabs
  with fava beans &
  anchovies 174
 grilled lamb cutlets with
  burnt butter, rosemary,
  anchovy & capers 167
 lamb meatballs with
  lemon & anchovies 175
 veal milanese with sage
  & anchovies 188, 199
apples

 pork with morcilla &
  apples 133, 145
 wild boar with apples
  222
apricots
 apricot & almond tart
  260, 275
 spiced lamb meatballs
  with apricots 175
 whole almond & apricot
  turron 281
artichoke
 artichoke with spicy
  lemon crumbs 239, 251
asparagus
 asparagus with spinach,
  garlic & pine nuts 240,
  252
 tempura asparagus with
  goat cheese & lavender
  honey 248

B

bacon
 beef carpaccio with
  parmesan, bacon,
  anchovy mayo & crispy
  garlic 193
 chicken cutlet with
  bacon & marsala 121
 roasted pheasant en
  cassoulet 206, 221
 see also pancetta
beans
 ballotine of rabbit &
  white beans 210, 223

 mallorcan slow-roasted
  lamb shoulder with
  white beans 168
 marinated lamb kebabs
  with zesty fava beans
  165, 174
 pork with morcilla, white
  beans & apples 145
 puree de habas 41, 60
 puree of white beans 60
 roasted pheasant en
  cassoulet 206, 221
 roast pork with fennel &
  betans 137, 147
beef
 beef carpaccio with
  anchovy mayo & crispy
  garlic 177, 193
 beef meatballs in spicy
  tomato sauce 144
 beef skewers with
  béarnaise sauce 180,
  195
 beef tenderloin with rioja
  & blue cheese 179, 194
 beef with potatoes, olives
  & sherry 122
 flap steak with bone
  marrow 184, 197
 grilled sirloin with
  porcini cream 191, 200
 hanger steak with
  celeriac & red cabbage
  192, 201
 ribeye with peppers &
  polenta fries 182, 196
 rich oxtail stew with

 parsnip puree 187, 198
 zamorano cheese &
  ground beef croquettas
  67
beets
 duck, beet & pickled
  walnut salad 116, 125
 warm lentils, goat's curd
  & beets 244, 255
berries
 panna cotta with
  gingered berries 278
blackberries
 venison with port,
  juniper, blackberries &
  cinnamon with celeriac
  puree 219
blue cheese
 beef tenderloin with rioja
  & blue cheese 179, 194
 duck, beet, blue cheese &
  pickled walnut salad
  125
 grilled sirloin with
  mushroom & stilton
  cream 200
 grilled sirloin with stilton
  cream sauce 200
boar
 wild boar with wild
  mushrooms 208, 222
bone marrow
 flap steak with bone
  marrow 184, 197
boquerones 24, 36
bread
 crispy eggs with wild

mushrooms & truffle 59, 69

goat cheese on toast with figs 47, 63

griddled sardines & rosemary salt 78, 94

pan con tomate 43, 61

seared foie gras with sherry-soaked raisins & sourdough toasts 217, 226

bruschetta 61

burrata cheese
puree de habas with burrata 60

C

cabbage
hanger steak with celeriac & red cabbage 192, 201

Calvados
calvados pollo a la ajillo 117

caperberries
see capers

capers 11
baked artichoke with capers & mint crumbs 251

charcuterie with pickled garlic & caperberries 20, 34

grilled lamb cutlets with burnt butter, rosemary & capers 151, 167

pork meatballs in tomato sauce with capers 144

sea bass tartare with dill & capers 66

veal milanese with sage

& capers 199

veal milanese with sage, capers & anchovies 199

cataplana 138

cavolo nero
roast chicken with truffle gnocchi, sage butter & cavolo nero 106, 120

celeriac
celeriac truffle gratin 241, 253

hanger steak with celeriac & red cabbage 192, 201

venison with port, juniper & cinnamon with celeriac puree 203, 219

chicken livers with pedro ximénez & chestnuts 224

cheeses
see individual entries

chestnuts
chicken livers with pedro ximénez & chestnuts 224

wild boar with wild mushrooms 208, 222

chicken
chicken cordon bleu goujons 104, 119

chicken cutlet with serrano ham & marsala 108, 121

chicken livers with pedro ximénez & iberico ham 213, 224

chicken pil pil 91

chicken pilaf 172

chicken wings with

honey & paprika 112, 123

chicken with potatoes, olives & sherry 111, 122

chicken with quince sauce 124

griddled chicken thighs with harissa, lime & garlic 103, 118

paella with seafood & chicken 86, 98

pollo a la ajillo 101, 117

roast chicken with truffle gnocchi, sage butter & cavolo nero 106, 120

roasted chicken en cassoulet 221

chickpeas
puree of chickpeas 60

chocolate
chocolate fondant 269, 279

chocolate natas 276

churros con chocolade 265, 277

white chocolate chocolate tart 280

chorizo 8
ballotine of rabbit with white beans, rosemary & chorizo 223

charcuterie with pickled garlic & caperberries 20, 34

chicken livers with pedro ximénez & chorizo 224

chorizo in red wine 127, 142

chorizo with spicy peppers & quail eggs 143

chorizo, morcilla & fennel sausages with sticky balsamic onions 141, 149

clams with chorizo, garlic & chile 82, 96

fried chorizo & potatoes 28, 38

mini chorizo & potato tortilla 247

paella with seafood & chicken 86, 98

PAN-FRIED PIMIENTOS DE PADRÓN WITH CHORIZO 37 [CHECK NAME]

patatas bravas with chorizo 246

pork stew with chorizo, garlic, wine & clams 148

pork stew with chorizo, saffron, garlic, wine & mussels 148

pork with chorizo & apples 145

roast pork with fennel, chorizo & beans 147

roasted pheasant en cassoulet with chorizo 221

scallops with chorizo & sage 97

churros
churros con chocolade 265, 277

clams
cataplana 138

clams with chorizo, garlic & chile 82, 96

paella with seafood &

chicken 86, 98
cod
  salt cod fritters with
    saffron aïoli 74, 92
  salt cod-stuffed piquillo
    peppers 30, 39
coffee
  coffee nadas 276
crab
  boiled artichoke filled
    with crabmeat salad
    251
  piquillo peppers stuffed
    with crabmeat 39
cream cheese
  zucchini flowers stuffed
    with peppered cream
    cheese & lavender
    honey 248
crème catalana 257, 273

D
duck
  duck breast with quince
    sauce 115, 124
  duck rillettes with
    membrillo 51, 65
  duck with pomegranate
    220
  duck, beet & pickled
    walnut salad 116, 125
  roast duck with
    pomegranate salad 171
dulce de leche
  churros con dulce de
    leche 277

E
eggs
  crispy eggs with wild
    mushrooms & truffle

59, 69
  morcilla with chanterelle
    mushrooms & duck
    eggs 143
  morcilla with spicy
    peppers & quail eggs
    129, 142
  veal milanese with egg,
    sage & anchovies 199
endive
  grilled belgian endive
    with walnuts &
    pomegranate seeds 243,
    254
equipment 12–15

F
fennel
  roast pork with fennel &
    beans 137, 147
feta cheese
  lamb meatballs with pine
    nuts & feta 175
  phyllo pastry with feta &
    spinach 236, 250
figs
  goat cheese on toast
    with figs 47, 63
foie gras
  see liver

G
garlic, pickled
  charcuterie with pickled
    garlic & caperberries
    20, 34
gnocchi
  roast chicken with truffle
    gnocchi, sage butter &
    cavolo nero 106, 120
goat cheese

duck, beet, goat cheese
  & pickled walnut salad
  125
  goat cheese on toast
    with figs 47, 63
  piquillo peppers stuffed
    with goat cheese 39
  pork & goat cheese
    goujons 119
  rib eye with piquillo
    peppers & goat cheese
    polenta fries 196
  warm lentils, goat's curd
    & beets 244, 255
  zucchini flowers stuffed
    with goat cheese &
    lavender honey 232,
    248
goat's curd
  see goat cheese
Gorgonzola cheese
  deep-fried stuffed olives
    with gorgonzola 64
grapes
  seared foie gras with
    grapes & sourdough
    toasts 226
guinea fowl
  guinea fowl with white
    beans 223
  guinea fowl, beet &
    pickled walnut salad
    125

H
halloumi cheese
  grilled belgian endive
    with grilled halloumi,
    lemon & pomegranate
    seeds 254
  warm lentils, grilled

halloumi & beets 255
ham
  calf's liver with baby
    onions, serrano & sweet
    sherry 214, 225
  charcuterie with pickled
    garlic & caperberries
    20, 34
  chicken cordon bleu
    goujons 104, 119
  chicken cutlet with
    serrano ham & marsala
    108, 121
  chicken livers with
    madeira & iberico ham
    224
  chicken livers with pedro
    ximénez & iberico ham
    213, 224
  goat cheese on toast
    with figs & ham63
  goat cheese on toast
    with serrano ham 63
  honey smoked ham
    goujons 119
  manchego & serrano
    croquettas 55, 67
  mozarella cheese on
    toast with figs &
    serrano ham63
  piquillo peppers stuffed
    with ham & rice 39
harissa
  griddled chicken thighs
    with harissa, lime &
    garlic 103, 118
  rose harissa marinated
    lamb kebabs & fava
    beans 174
hazelnuts
  asparagus with spinach,

garlic & hazelnuts 252

J

juniper berries
  venison with port,
    juniper & cinnamon
    with celeriac puree 203,
    219

L

lamb
  grilled lamb cutlets with
    burnt butter, rosemary
    & capers 151, 167
  harissa lamb cutlets 118
  lamb fillet with tzatziki
    154, 169
  lamb pilaf 161, 172
  lamb ragout with polenta
    156, 170
  mallorcan slow-roasted
    lamb shoulder 153, 168
  marinated lamb kebabs
    with zesty fava beans
    165, 174
  pan fried lamb cutlets
    with herbed bread
    crumbs 162, 173
  roast lamb with
    pomegranate salad 158,
    171
  spiced lamb meatballs
    with crushed pistachios
    166, 176
lentils
  ballotine of rabbit with
    lentils 223
  warm lentils, goat's curd
    & beets 244, 255
liver
  chicken livers with pedro

ximénez & iberico ham
    213, 224
  seared foie gras with
    sherry-soaked raisins &
    sourdough toasts 217,
    226
lobster
  paella with seafood,
    lobster & chicken 98

M

mackerel
  griddled mackerel &
    rosemary salt 94
  mackerel tartare with
    horseradish 52, 66
  warm lentils, smoked
    mackerel, goat's curd &
    beets 255
Madeira
  chicken livers with
    madeira & iberico ham
    224
Manchego cheese
  chicken cordon bleu
    goujons 104, 119
  manchego & serrano
    croquettes 55, 67
  marinated manchego
    with peppers & cumin
    23, 35
mango
  pork ribs in mango-
    adobo barbecue sauce
    146
Marsala
  chicken cutlet with
    serrano ham & marsala
    108, 121
membrillo 8
  duck rillettes with

membrillo 51, 65
monkfish
  griddled monkfish with
    garlic, orange & smoked
    paprika 95
  monkfish pil pil 91
morcilla 11
  chorizo, morcilla &
    fennel sausages with
    sticky balsamic onions
    141, 149
  morcilla in red wine 142
  morcilla with spicy
    peppers & quail eggs
    129, 142
  patatas bravas with
    blood sausage 246
  pork with morcilla &
    apples 133, 145
  scallops with blood
    sausages & sage 85, 97
mortadella
  charcuterie with
    mortadella, truffle
    cheese & pistachios 34
mozzarella cheese
  mozzarella cheese on
    toast with figs 63
  mozzarella cheese on
    toast with figs &
    serrano ham63
mullet
  griddled mullet &
    rosemary salt 94
mushrooms
  crispy eggs with wild
    mushrooms & truffle
    59, 69
  grilled sirloin with
    porcini cream 191, 200
  morcilla with chanterelle

mushrooms & duck
    eggs 143
  mushrooms in garlic &
    herbs 234, 249
  wild boar with wild
    mushrooms 208, 222
mussels
  pork stew with chorizo,
    saffron, garlic, wine &
    mussels 148

N

natas 262, 76

O

olives
  anchovy & olive
    tapenade 44, 62
  chicken with potatoes,
    olives & sherry 111, 122
  deep fried stuffed olives
    48, 64
  lamb meatballs with
    kalamata olives 175
  marinated olives 17, 32
  pork meatballs in tomato
    sauce with olives 144
oranges
  chocolate orange
    fondant 279
  churros con chocolade
    with orange 277
  griddled calamari with
    garlic, orange & smoked
    paprika 81, 95
  orange crème catalana
    273
  orange custard tart 270,
    280
  quail with orange &
    pomegranate 220

quail with orange 220
roast lamb with
  pomegranate & orange
  salad 171
ouzo
  mallorcan slow-roasted
    lamb shoulder with
    ouzo 168 [corrected
    from "orzo"]
oxtail
  rich oxtail stew with
    parsnip puree 187, 198

P

paella
  black paella with garlic
    squid 89, 99
  paella with seafood &
    chicken 86, 98
pancetta
  ballotine of rabbit &
    white beans 210, 223
  calf's liver with baby
    onions, pancetta &
    sweet sherry 224
  flap steak with pancetta
    & bone marrow 197
  roast pork with fennel,
    pancetta & beans 147
  scallops with pancetta &
    sage 97
  sweetbreads with
    pancetta & pedro
    xiemenez 227
Parmesan cheese
  artichoke with spicy
    lemon crumbs 239, 251
  beef carpaccio with
    parmesan, anchovy
    mayo & crispy garlic
    193

beef carpaccio with
  parmesan, bacon,
  anchovy mayo & crispy
  garlic 193
classic beef carpaccio
  193
crispy eggs with wild
  mushrooms, parmesan
  & truffle 69
croquettas with spinach
  56, 68
deep-fried stuffed olives
  with Parmesan 64
lamb ragout with polenta
  156, 170
ribeye with peppers &
  polenta fries 182, 196
roast chicken with truffle
  gnocchi, sage butter &
  cavolo nero 106, 120
parsnips
  rich oxtail stew with
    parsnip puree 187, 198
pastry
  apricot & almond tart
    260, 275
  natas 262, 76
  orange custard tart 270,
    280
  phyllo pastry with feta &
    spinach 236, 250
pâté
  pâté charcuterie with
    pickled garlic &
    caperberries 34
peaches
  panna cotta with roasted
    peaches 278
pears
  pear & almond tart 275
  pork with chorizo &

pears 145
pork with morcilla &
  pears 145
Pedro Ximénez
see sherry
peppers
  charcuterie with red
    peppers & arugula 34
  marinated manchego
    with peppers & cumin
    23, 35
  pan-fried pimientos de
    padrón 27, 37
  pimientos de padrón 8
  piquillo peppers 8
  salt cod-stuffed piquillo
    peppers 30, 39
  morcilla with spicy
    peppers & quail eggs
    129, 142
  ribeye with peppers &
    polenta fries 182, 196
pheasant
  roasted pheasant en
    cassoulet 206, 221
pine nuts
  asparagus with spinach,
    garlic & pine nuts 240,
    252
  grilled red endive with
    pine nuts &
    pomegranate seeds 254
  lamb meatballs with pine
    nuts & feta 175
pineapple
  pork ribs in pineapple-
    adobo barbecue sauce
    146
pistachios
  apricot & pistachio tart
    275

charcuterie with
  mortadella, truffle
  cheese & pistachios 34
pistachio turron 281
rice pudding with
  pistachios &
  pomegranate-rosewater
  syrup 259, 274
spiced lamb meatballs
  with crushed pistachios
  166, 176
plums
  panna cotta with roasted
    plums 278
  plum & almond tart 275
polenta
  lamb ragout with polenta
    156, 170
  ribeye with peppers &
    polenta fries 182, 196
  rich oxtail stew with
    polenta 198
pomegranate
  grilled belgian endive
    with walnuts &
    pomegranate seeds 243,
    254
  quail with pomegranate
    205, 220
  rice pudding with
    pistachios &
    pomegranate-rosewater
    syrup 259, 274
  roast lamb with
    pomegranate salad 158,
    171
pork
  cataplana 138
  pork & goat cheese
    goujons 119
  pork meatballs in tomato

sauce 130, 144
pork ribs in adobo
    barbecue sauce 134,
    146
pork rillettes with
    membrillo 65
pork tenderloin with
    rioja & blue cheese 194
pork with morcilla &
    apples 133, 145
roast pork with fennel &
    beans 137, 147
Port
chicken livers with port
    & pancetta 224
chicken with potatoes,
    olives & port 122
pollo a la ajillo with port
    117
venison with port,
    juniper & cinnamon
    with celeriac puree 203,
    219
potatoes
chicken with potatoes,
    olives & sherry 111, 122
fried chorizo & potatoes
    28, 38
lamb ragout with creamy
    mashed potatoes 170
mini tortilla 231, 247
patatas bravas 229, 246
prawns
gambas pil pil 73, 91
king prawns with garlic
    & smoked paprika 77,
    93
prunes
lamb pilaf with prunes
    172
pumpkin seeds

roasted almonds & seeds
    19, 33

Q
quail
quail with pomegranate
    205, 220
quince
duck breast with quince
    sauce 115, 124
see also membrillo

R
rabbit
ballotine of rabbit &
    white beans 210, 223
conejo a la ajillo 117
paella with seafood &
    rabbit 98
raisins
seared foie gras with
    sherry-soaked raisins &
    sourdough toasts 217,
    226
raspberries
chocolate raspberry
    fondant with vanilla ice
    cream 279
raspberry & almond tart
    275
rhubarb
panna cotta with roasted
    rhubarb 266, 278
ricotta cheese
deep fried stuffed olives
    48, 64
phyllo pastry with feta &
    spinach 236, 250
rosewater
cardamon & rosewater
    nadas 276

rice pudding with
    pistachios &
    pomegranate–rosewater
    syrup 259, 274

S
saffron 8
chorizo & chile in white
    wine & saffron 142
pork stew with chorizo,
    saffron, garlic, wine &
    mussels 148
pork stew with saffron,
    garlic, wine & clams
    148
salt cod fritters with
    saffron aïoli 74, 92
salami
salami charcuterie with
    pickled garlic &
    caperberries 34
salmon
salmon tartare with
    horseradish 66
salt cod
see cod
sardines
boquerones 24, 36
griddled sardines &
    rosemary salt 78, 94
sausage
ballotine of rabbit with
    white beans, rosemary,
    pancetta & sausage 223
charcuterie with pickled
    garlic & caperberries
    20, 34
chorizo, morcilla &
    fennel sausages with
    sticky balsamic onions
    141, 149

roasted pheasant &
    toulouse sausage en
    cassoulet 221
scallops with garlic
    sausages & sage 97
sausage, blood
see morcilla
scallops
fritto misto with scallops
    90
scallops with blood
    sausages & sage 85, 97
sea bass
sea bass tartare with dill
    & capers 66
sesame seeds
sesame beef skewers with
    béarnaise sauce 195
sherry 11
calf's liver with baby
    onions, serrano & sweet
    sherry 214, 225
chicken livers with pedro
    ximénez & iberico ham
    213, 224
chicken with potatoes,
    olives & sherry 111, 122
seared foie gras with
    sherry-soaked raisins &
    sourdough toasts 217,
    226
sweetbreads with pedro
    ximénez 218, 227
vinegar 11
shrimp
fritto misto 71, 90
manchego & shrimp
    croquettas 67
paella with seafood &
    chicken 86, 98
piquillo peppers stuffed

with shrimp 39
shrimp fritters with
saffron aïoli 92
smelts
fritto misto 71, 90
smoked paprika 8
griddled calamari with
garlic, orange & smoked
paprika 81, 95
king prawns with garlic
& smoked paprika 77,
93
spinach
asparagus with spinach,
garlic & pine nuts 240,
252
croquettas with spinach
56, 68
phyllo pastry with feta &
spinach 236, 250
black paella with garlic
squid 89, 99
squid
fritto misto 71, 90
griddled calamari with
garlic, orange & smoked
paprika 81, 95
paella with seafood &
chicken 86, 98
Stilton
see blue cheese
stout
stout-braised oxtail with
parsnip puree 198
sunflower seeds
roasted almonds & seeds
19, 33
sweetbreads
sweetbreads with pedro
ximénez 218, 227

T
toffee
chocolate toffee fondant
with vanilla ice cream
279
tortilla
mini tortilla 231, 247
truffle cheese
charcuterie with
mortadella, truffle
cheese & pistachios 34
truffle
celeriac truffle gratin
241, 253
crispy eggs with wild
mushrooms & truffle
59, 69
croquettas with four
cheeses & truffle 68
croquettas with spinach
& truffle 68
flap steak & truffle 197
morcilla with crisp sage,
duck eggs & truffle oil
143
roast chicken with truffle
gnocchi, sage butter &
cavolo nero 106, 120
seared foie gras with
sherry-soaked raisins,
truffle & sourdough
toasts 226
tuna
tuna tartare with
avocado 66
turkey
turkey meatballs in
tomato sauce with basil
144
turron 272, 281

V
veal
calf's liver with baby
onions, serrano & sweet
sherry 214, 225
sweetbreads with pedro
ximénez 218, 227
veal cordon bleu goujons
119
veal cutlet with serrano
ham & marsala 121
veal milanese with sage
& anchovies 188, 199
venison
venison skewers with
béarnaise sauce
venison tenderloin with
rioja & blue cheese 194
venison tenderloin with
rioja & goat cheese 194
venison with port,
juniper & cinnamon
with celeriac puree 203,
219
venison with wild
mushrooms 222
vermouth
chicken cutlet with
serrano ham &
vermouth 121
grilled sirloin with
vermouth & porcini
cream 200

W
walnuts
duck, beet & pickled
walnut salad 116, 125
grilled belgian endive
with walnuts &
pomegranate seeds 243,
254
quail with pomegranate
& walnut 220
roasted walnuts, seeds &
apricots 33
scared foie gras with
sherry-soaked raisins,
pickled walnuts &
sourdough toasts 226
whitebait
fritto misto 71, 90
wine
beef tenderloin with rioja
& blue cheese 179, 194
chorizo in red wine 127,
142
chorizo, morcilla &
fennel sausages with
sticky wine onions 149
lamb ragout with red
wine & polenta 170
lamb ragout with
tomatoes & white wine
with polenta 170
mallorcan slow-roasted
lamb shoulder with red
wine 168

Z
Zamorano cheese
zamorano cheese &
ground beef croquettas
67
zucchini
zucchini flowers stuffed
with goat cheese &
lavender honey 232,
248
zucchini with spinach,
garlic & pine nuts 252